LESSONS LEARNED

A Guide to Accident Prevention and Crisis Response

University of Alaska Anchorage
Alaska Outdoor & Experiential Education

Alaska Outdoor & Experiential Education
University of Alaska Anchorage
3211 Providence Drive, Anchorage, Alaska 99508
Find us on the web: www.uaa.alaska.edu/aoee

Editor: Deborah Ajango
Associate Editors: Kay Landis and Shannon Gramse
Cover and Typesetting Design: Judy Edwards
Printing and Binding: Northern Printing, Anchorage, Alaska 99518
Front Cover Photograph: Descending Karsten's Ridge, Brian Okonek
Back Cover Photographs: Wading McKinley River, Brian Okonek;
Two on Rock Face © Brad Wrobleski/Masterfile;
Whitewater Rafting, PhotoDisc
Black and White Photographs: Brian Okonek, James Larabee, and PhotoDisc

Printed in the United States of America

ISBN 0-9702845-0-0

LESSONS LEARNED:
A Guide to Accident Prevention and Crisis Response

"*Lessons Learned* is comprehensive in its look at the design and delivery of outdoor adventure programs from the standpoint of managing the risks to participants. In clear, compelling terms, the authors provide insight and guidance gained from many decades of experience as instructors and program leaders. This is an invaluable guide for field and management staff, whether new or seasoned."

Lewis Glenn
Vice President, Safety and Program
Outward Bound USA

"This is an important book for emerging leaders in the field of outdoor pursuits. Early in my career there certainly were times when I could have used the information and perspectives found in each chapter. I look forward to having it available to our students."

John E. (Jed) Williamson
President, Sterling College
Editor, *Accidents in North America Mountaineering*

"If you think a serious incident or accident 'could never happen to me,' you need to stop what you are doing, sit down and read this book. If you are not moved by what it says, then perhaps you should choose another career."

Bill Zimmerman
Accreditation Coordinator
Association for Experiential Education

I owe tremendous thanks to the many people who helped make this book possible.

First, to Provost Dan Johnson, for the desire and commitment to see this happen, and to the University of Alaska Anchorage for all the support that was provided.

To the authors, who agreed to help with this project simply because they believed in the cause; to Jed Williamson, for his feedback and contribution to this volume, and for his incredible commitment to the betterment of the industry; and to Reb Gregg, for the expertise he added to chapters one and four.

To Kay Landis, associate editor, who had a vision and provided energy from the start. Without her, this book would not be nearly as complete as it is. To Shannon Gramse, associate editor, for his ideas, additions, and style expertise.

To Judy Edwards, for the many hours she provided in layout, production and design. To Brian Okonek and James Larabee for the use of their photographs throughout the book; and to Ron Spatz, for his helpful advice.

To the office staff at AOEE, and to the numerous friends and colleagues from near and far who contributed by proofreading various chapters and providing many other forms of assistance.

On June 29, 1997, a group of 12 beginning mountaineering students and two instructors from the University of Alaska Anchorage was involved in a tragic climbing accident just east of Anchorage. Descending a snow-filled gully from the 4,880-foot summit of Ptarmigan Peak on a beautiful summer afternoon, a student on the highest rope team slipped and was unable to self-arrest. When he reached the end of his rope, the force of the impact knocked his teammates from their stances, even though they were using their ice axes as anchors. The top team fell into the rope team below, causing a chain reaction. Within seconds, all 14 climbers were swept nearly 1,000 feet down the 30-40 degree slope. Before the day was over, two students had died and many others were seriously injured.

How could such a thing happen and what exactly went wrong? These were the questions everyone was asking in the aftermath of the fall. Although the university had a response plan in place, it was not fully prepared to deal with such a catastrophic event. The media and public wanted answers that the university was unable to provide.

The university community was torn by the tragedy. Aching with compassion for the injured climbers and their families, recognizing their responsibility to answer the community's concerns about what went wrong, and struggling themselves to understand how such a thing could happen, administrators also faced legal liability issues. The advice of counsel was to err on the side of caution when it came to releasing information. As the days and then weeks passed, however, the demand for an explanation grew. Yet for a long time—some would say too long—there was little to share.

It took a special task-force review, a series of community forums, an external investigation, and a year of agonized soul-searching before all the questions surrounding the accident and university's outdoor program were answered effectively. The investigative team concluded that while adequate instruction had been given up to the day of the climb, mistakes had been made on Ptarmigan Peak. The group should have chosen an easily accessed, non-technical route rather than use the gully for their descent, the report concluded. Further, the descent technique chosen by the instructors was inappropriate for the conditions of the snow, the steepness of the terrain, and the abilities of the students. Fatigue, inadequate footwear, and the lack of a safe run-out may have been contributing factors as well. The report recommended suspension of the mountaineering courses while the department reevaluated its practices.

After the accident, the outdoor program itself wanted not only to learn how such a fall could have happened, but it was committed to addressing other, equally important questions as well: what went wrong with the system, and how could it guard against a similar accident happening in the future? Over the next 18 months, the department initiated a comprehensive review process that would examine not just its mountaineering course but every aspect of its programming. As a result, substantial changes were made: policies and procedures were modified; the department renewed and strengthened its commitment to safety; and in the end, it changed its name to Alaska Outdoor & Experiential Education, a title that more accurately reflects its mission and direction.

It is rarely easy to know exactly *why* accidents happen. But if there's anything at all to be gained from a tragedy like Ptarmigan Peak, it is the painful yet enlightening lessons that people learn along the way: *how* do accidents happen, what can be done to prevent them, and how can an organization respond effectively should the unthinkable occur?

This book is our attempt to share some of that experience and knowledge. Using Ptarmigan Peak and other case studies as examples, we hope to help outdoor educators benefit from the collective experience of a number of professionals. We offer this information as a stimulus for discussion and a guide to accident prevention and crisis response.

Ed.

The impetus for this volume comes from the deep institutional desire at the University of Alaska Anchorage to fully understand the factors that contributed to the Ptarmigan Peak accident. Equally important is the sense of obligation to apply and share that understanding to enhance safety in outdoor experiential education. One of the outcomes of the accident and its aftermath has been the growing sense of mission to actively contribute to the knowledge-base on mountaineering safety and other issues associated with the outdoor education industry.

The title of this book, *Lessons Learned*, is a bold statement that suggests some measure of success in acquiring increased knowledge worthy of sharing to the broader community. It is our hope that the original papers that make up this volume will stimulate even stronger commitments to enhanced safety by furthering the dialogue among educators, administrators, managers, and trustees of experiential educational institutions. Likewise, it is our hope that we, as a university community, have also been a *learning community* and that we did, indeed, learn from the many lessons such a tragic experience provides.

Nearly a decade ago Peter M. Senge wrote about learning organizations in his influential book, *The Fifth Discipline: The Art and Practice of the Learning Organization* (1990). For Senge, learning organizations are organizations where "people continually expand their capacity to create the results they truly desire, where new and expansive patterns of thinking are nurtured, where collective aspiration is set free, and where people are continually learning how to learn together" (p. 3).

In the weeks, months, and now years following the Ptarmigan Peak accident, we have strived to become that learning organization. The university and the Alaska mountaineering community probed a host of factors that were seen as potentially relevant to the fatal fall. We reviewed, studied, investigated, and researched the conditions, equipment, descent techniques, skill levels, mental and physical states of the climbers and instructors, program policies and protocols, managerial structure and practices, and decision-making processes. Have we, as a result of these substantial and continuing efforts, learned how to learn together? Have we freed our collective aspirations to design and develop powerful but equally safe outdoor experiential educational programs and courses? Have we encouraged new patterns of thinking that will enhance learning and safety? And has the knowledge gained strengthened our resolve to provide highly effective learning opportunities and experiences with an appropriate level of risk?

These questions—and the lessons from the past three years—are not only for the instructors and managers of outdoor education programs but are for all levels of an institution. At the University of Alaska Anchorage, offices of the dean, provost, chancellor, university relations, legal counsel, risk management, president, and the Board of Regents have been and will continue to be challenged by the very nature of, and inherent risks associated with, active learning and experiential education. As instruction increasingly moves from the relative safety of the classroom into the community, the outdoors, and to foreign countries, universities and other educational institutions must themselves become practitioners of lifelong learning. To be successful, institutions may need to reassess lines of communication and hierarchical organizational structures and place even greater emphasis on teams, dialogue, and listening to help foster learning in the organization.

One of the many things I learned during the past three years is that those who engage in mountaineering and outdoor education constitute a "community." Those who have contributed to this volume are members of that community and, as members, speak the language of outdoor educators. Some of what is written here may not be new to this community; the challenge then, may be to communicate with those who are not members of this order but who have a need—and indeed a responsibility—to learn from the lessons that confront experiential educators on a daily basis.

In an earlier report on the Ptarmigan Peak accident, we pledged to learn from this tragic experience (June 17, 1998).

It is my hope and expectation that *Lessons Learned* reflects progress toward this goal, and that it will help meet the growing need for greater communication among all the stakeholders in outdoor experiential education.

Daniel M. Johnson
Provost
University of Alaska Anchorage
July 2000

LESSONS LEARNED:

A Guide to Accident Prevention
and Crisis Response

16,200 feet on Denali

R*Risk management* has become something of an industry buzzword in recent years. The presence of risk is a defining feature of the outdoor education/adventure industry, and the management of those risks is one of our greatest challenges. But even within the industry, not everyone uses the expression to mean the same thing. Program managers, insurance adjusters, trip leaders, and lawyers all tend to focus on different aspects of this complex topic.

Most outdoor organizations stress accident prevention as the primary goal of their risk management plans. They buy the highest quality equipment, hire the most experienced instructors or guides, and keep student-to-instructor ratios low, hoping to avoid accidents altogether. If they do everything right, they reason, it will never happen to them. But accidents do occur, even with the best-laid plans.

This book takes the position that effective risk management involves more than just having a good safety record. An effective plan includes steps that should be taken before and during all outings as well as damage control steps that can be followed after an accident. The definition we have adopted comes from consultant Ian Wade (1999): Risk management is the process of reducing the potential for incidents to an acceptable level and minimizing the consequences to the people and the organization in the event an accident occurs.

The approach we recommend, therefore, is multifaceted. An agency should constantly brainstorm all of the "what ifs" that might possibly go wrong, and should take steps to minimize the probability that an unwelcome or unexpected event will occur. A risk management plan should also include solid crisis response planning to keep damage to a minimum once an incident happens. Not only should instructors be trained in wilderness first aid and crisis response, for instance, but an organization should have plans for getting injured and non-injured people out of the field; for notifying family members; and for communicating with the media in a language that laymen, unfamiliar with the outdoor industry's nomenclature, can understand. Lastly, an effective plan will include a systematic assessment of whether the prevention strategies and emergency action plans are up to date and working appropriately.

This book presents insights from nine authors who each approach risk management from a different point of view. The authors include accident investigators, field instructors and educators, administrators, a defense attorney, and a TV newsman. The lessons they discuss are intended for trip leaders, program managers, and anyone who is considering a career in the outdoor education/adventure industry.

Drew Leemon and Scott Erickson, each of whom has investigated and studied dozens of accidents, start by taking a look at the causes of accidents. Using case studies of real accidents as examples, the authors identify contributing factors that are common to many mishaps and tragedies.

Simon Priest and Deb Ajango offer steps that can minimize the probability of an accident or incident. Priest, nationally known for his research and writing on effective leadership, discusses the role of instructor judgment in accident prevention and suggests ways to help improve judgment in outdoor leaders. Ajango, manager of a university outdoor education program, contends that it isn't enough to simply "hire the best." She describes key components that should be included in an organization's prevention plan, including the appropriate place for and use of policies and procedures.

Attorney Bob Hicks discusses several steps that instructors and agencies can take to minimize their exposure to legal liability. He and attorney Reb Gregg also provide advice for orchestrating an accident-response plan so that it appropriately addresses the needs of the victim(s) as well as the organization.

Television producer Ty Hardt offers a reporter's perspective on how to work with the media before and after an incident. He believes it is essential to build a relationship with the media now, and have a media response plan in place and ready to go on a moment's notice.

In a topic fundamental to all outdoor programs, Jasper Hunt addresses the ethics of exposing people to risk. Knowing that accidents can and will happen in the industry,

Hunt addresses some of the difficult ethical questions that outdoor leaders, managers, and administrators must face daily.

Lastly, Conni Livsey and Bill Ennis, experienced leaders and long-time outdoor instructors, discuss the importance of ongoing assessment in the management of risk. By examining the evolution of an outdoor program over a 25-year period, they describe how change, though inevitable, can be difficult and even dangerous if not confronted and negotiated.

Taken together, this information can help outdoor education/adventure agencies—big or small—create or improve their risk management plans. The broad range of topics and the many different points of view provide the reader with theoretical insight and practical advice that can be used before or after an incident occurs.

When things do not go as planned, people are often quick to point fingers. It is usually easier to find fault than to find meaning, especially when mistakes have been made. Although placing blame may be human nature, and anger may be an essential part of healing, it is important that we move beyond condemning, learn from the past and improve where we can.

As Jasper Hunt says in Chapter Six, "An accident that might be deemed tolerable is one … from which great learning takes place, where people think about things they may not have thought about before, where the balance between risk and benefit is examined, where the continued welfare of our students is held as a sacred trust."

This book is dedicated to all students and leaders who have ever been injured or killed during their pursuit of adventure and as a consequence of their love of the outdoors. The information presented here provides an opportunity to learn from their experiences so that others may benefit in the future.

Finally, may we always remember that little can be learned if our final words are, "That never would have happened to me."

How Accidents Happen

By Drew Leemon and Scott Erickson © 2000

This chapter explores the current state of thinking on how accidents happen in outdoor adventure activities. The authors explain several methods for analyzing accidents and use real case studies to demonstrate the practical applications of these methods. Accident data are used to determine and categorize the types and causes of accidents, which in turn, can provide the catalyst for improvement.

At first glance, it seems easy enough to say how an outdoor adventure accident happened.[1] A climber dies after falling off the mountain, a river kayaker drowns in a whitewater rapid, a backpacker fractures his leg descending a steep snow-covered slope. But this level of description is really only a statement of the end result. It tells us *what* happened without explaining *how* it happened.

The true nature of an accident is almost always far more complex. Upon analysis, most accidents do not turn out to be simple isolated events, random occurrences, or mere bad luck. Nor do they result from a single-cause factor. The slip or fall might be considered a primary cause, but causal theories also include a variety of other terms such as proximate cause, basic cause, root cause, probable cause, direct cause, contributing cause, and underlying cause to describe the multitude of factors that can contribute to an accident. There is no universal agreement regarding which terms are most useful; however, those who study accidents generally agree

[1] *The terms incident and accident are used interchangeably throughout this book.*

ac•ci•dent\n *1) a: an unforeseen and unplanned event or circumstance b: lack of intention or necessity: CHANCE, <met by ~ rather than by design> 2) a: an unfortunate event resulting especially from carelessness or ignorance b: an unexpected happening causing loss or injury which is not due to any fault or misconduct on the part of the person injured but for which legal relief may be sought.*

about one thing. Most accidents include a series of interrelated environmental conditions, actions, and human decisions that in combination lead to an unexpected, unintended, and sometimes tragic result.

In general, outdoor adventure accidents happen through the interplay of three main factors. The first is environmental: the powerful, unforgiving forces of the natural world, such as weather, gravity, or strong currents. The second is the adventurer's desire to seek outdoor activities and challenges. It is this desire that brings people to place themselves (either knowingly or unknowingly) in risky situations. The third factor is the way people make decisions about the risks and hazards they encounter, a process that depends on experience, judgment, and emotion. We learn how accidents happen by investigating and analyzing them in relation to these three categories.

The mere presence of all three factors doesn't guarantee that an accident will happen; the interrelationship between exposure to hazards, human performance, and decision-making only creates the potential that one might occur. Even the most extreme combinations that create a possibility of an accident —aerial combat missions, for instance—have ended with fine results. Given the same basic set of circumstances in two separate scenarios, a tiny change in just one element may lead to completely different outcomes.

No organization can ever achieve total control over all the factors that might cause an accident. Hazards can be moderated but never eliminated. In mathematical terms, the probability of causal elements combining in an accident sequence is always greater than one. For this reason, accidents by themselves are a poor indication of an organization's general health. "Safe" organizations can still have bad accidents, while "unsafe" ones can escape them for long periods of time. In other words, one should not conclude that the organization with zero accidents is somehow safe all the time.

If we can neither predict accidents nor completely control them, then why bother to study them at all? What's there to learn from the investigation of an accident, besides, of course, who is to blame?

"Safe" organizations can still have bad accidents, while "unsafe" ones can escape them for long periods of time.

A post-accident investigation is used to discover the particular sequence of how an accident happened. By identifying the sequence of events, it reveals possible turning points all along the way, small changes that might have led to a completely different outcome. Understanding the full complexity of the event can help reveal countermeasures that might have prevented it or that might have mitigated its consequences. Accident investigations, therefore, provide a road map for learning how risk management strategies can be improved. Risk assessment and risk management strategies, in turn, can be used by organizations to counter, or mitigate, the potential for accidents.

A determination of cause may serve other useful purposes as well, including standardizing terms, and providing a statistical database for analysis, observation of trends, and prediction of future problem areas. Causes in themselves serve no purpose unless some preventative action is taken; they can even be counterproductive if the goal of an investigation is merely to find someone to blame. The ultimate goal of safety managers and investigators is not to assign blame but to reduce the potential for future accidents.

Understanding Accidents

Almost every situation in the outdoors contains the potential for an accident. When we combine a novice climber with unfamiliar equipment and an instructor who has to provide supervision from the end of a 50-meter climbing rope, for instance, the chance of a mishap can be quite high. A common type of incident that occurs in educational climbing programs is illustrated in the following example.

In the Wind River Mountains of Wyoming, a student on a backcountry rock-climbing course took off her climbing harness as the climbing party crossed some third-class (easy) terrain. When she put her harness back on to finish the fifth-class (technical) portion of the climb, she failed to attach the leg loops to the waist belt. A little later, while on a top belay, she fell. She hung for approximately 30 minutes before an instructor could descend to assist her. At that time, he observed her improperly attached harness and corrected the problem. The student later complained of soreness to her lower front rib cage, but fortunately there was no injury or lasting damage. This seemingly small mistake could have resulted in asphyxiation or damage to her internal organs.

Another example of an incident that didn't result in injury occurred on the Clearwater River in Alaska. It was the 71st day of a 75-day-long expedition. A group of four students and one instructor decided to wade across the river, holding hands and crossing as a chain. As part of the group reached the swiftest part of the current, one student fell, which caused everyone else to lose their balance as well. The student leading the chain quickly scrambled out of the river, and two other students and the instructor were able to get out shortly thereafter.

The first student to fall down was not so lucky. Although she had unfastened her backpack's waist belt before the crossing, she had forgotten to unclip her sternum strap. In her struggle to get her pack off, she began to be carried off by the current. She floated sideways facing the opposite bank with her head above water for about 100 yards before the instructor and another student were able to get to her from the bank and help her from the river. They all warmed themselves by changing clothes and hiking the remaining two miles to camp. Although people got wet and cold, no one was seriously hurt.

These incidents are what we would call near misses or close calls: accidents in which no injury occurs even though the potential for serious injury is high. They illustrate how several elements combine within a sequence of events to produce an accidental outcome. Subtle changes in any of the events might have led to a different end result or to a different weighting or arrangement of causal and contributing factors. In other words, identification of the causal factors, and removal of any one of them, might prevent an accident from happening.

Some safety experts have defined an accident as being driven by two main factors: unsafe acts and unsafe conditions. The Dynamics of Accidents Theory was developed by Alan Hale, one of the first people to apply accident theory to outdoor adventure programming (1983). The theory organizes causal factors into two broad categories: 1) objective factors, which are the ones we usually cannot control, and 2) subjective factors, which we can control to a certain extent. These two categories of accident factors exist separately and at times interact to create what is referred to as the *accident potential.*

As illustrated in Figure 1.1, the greater the interaction of

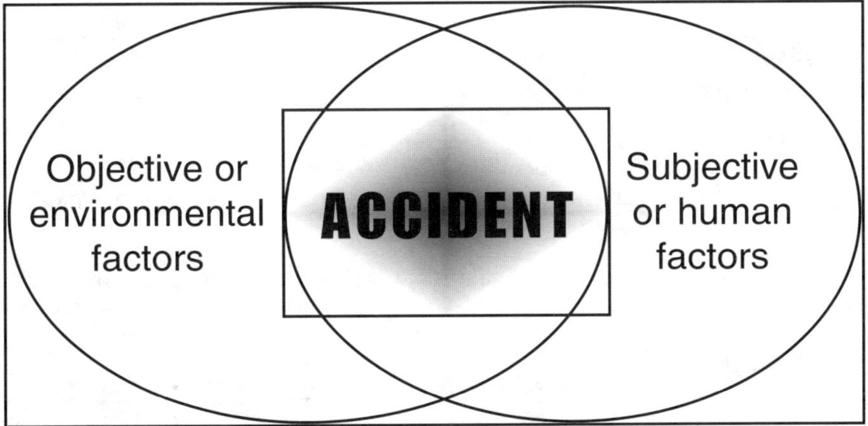

Figure 1.1 *The greatest potential for accidents occurs when objective and subjective factors overlap or interact. (Adapted from Hale's 1983 work.)*

the objective and subjective factors, the greater the potential for an accident to occur.

Figure 1.2 lists the objective and subjective factors associated with crossing a river such as the Clearwater. An examination of these factors along with the specific conditions on the river that day can lead to a determination of contributing causes.

Objective Factors	Subjective Factors
The depth/current of the river; water temperature	Ability of each group member to wade this river
The time of day	The group's knowledge of river crossing methods
The type of riverbed (mud, sand, rocks, etc.)	The experience level of the group in crossing rivers of this size and type
Affects on river level: snowmelt/rainfall	The group: fresh, rested, and hydrated?
Geography of the watershed	The group: tired, hungry, and cold?
Presence or absence of bridges either man-made or natural	Alternatives to crossing the river
Presence or absence of downstream hazards such as rapids, waterfalls, or sweepers	Alternatives to crossing at this spot
Entry and exit points	Communication within the group
Weather: temperature, precipitation, wind, etc.	Awareness of the hazard

Figure 1.2 *This analysis of the Clearwater River incident breaks down relevant hazards into subjective and objective factors.*

At the end of the expedition, an analysis of the Clearwater River incident identified the following factors as contributing causes:

- The group was "heading for the barn." The expedition was almost over and students were complacent about the seriousness of this river crossing.
- The group underestimated the hazard, thinking that the Clearwater River was easy and that the "real" challenge on this route was the McKinley River.
- The clear water and easily visible river bottom further diminished the hazard in their minds.
- The group should have scouted the crossing site more carefully. The simple act of scouting can heighten your awareness and get group members to focus on the hazard.
- Instructor supervision was inadequate. The instructor was conflicted between letting the students lead and make their own decisions and knowing how to effectively "pull the plug" or intervene when he thought the students were making unsafe decisions. The instructor was concerned about not being condescending to the students and allowing for their learning experience.

In this case the river was the objective factor, but it certainly didn't cause the accident. The subjective factors of the students' complacency (including a lack of awareness of the extent of the hazard presented by the river) and the group's unclear expectations of when the instructor should intervene both contributed to the accident.

Using a slightly different set of factors, James Reason (1991) describes accidents as latent failures in managerial and organizational arenas that combine adversely with local triggering events (weather, location, etc.) and with active failures of individuals (errors and procedural violations). He describes an organizational accident as consisting of three elements: an organizational process, task and environmental conditions, and at the individual level, a variety of potentially unsafe acts.

The Clearwater River incident can be analyzed using Reason's concept of organizational accidents as well. The expedition was part of a wilderness education program designed to teach leadership. This was its organizational arena. The task consisted of two parts: 1) to cross the river to get to camp, and 2) to provide practical leadership experience. The environmental conditions included the river and its cold, swift water. And there were a variety of unsafe acts, including one student's failure to unfasten her sternum strap and the whole group's complacency regarding the hazard.

We can use our analysis of this accident and our understanding of the subjective and objective contributing factors to imagine how the accident might have been prevented. The prevention of accidents in outdoor adventure programming relies heavily on the leaders' and participants' understanding of the interplay of these factors and their ability to evaluate hazards within this framework.

To illustrate, picture a high school backpacking class with eight students and two leaders. On the seventh day of a 10-day trip, the group encounters a 30-foot-wide river with a four-mile-per-hour current and no bridge. Their scheduled pick-up is on the morning of the 10th day at a road head, 15 miles beyond the river. From an initial attempt to wade across, they learn that the river is at least three feet deep and possibly deeper.

This situation sets the scene for a potential accident.

The degree to which the river presents a danger is related to the many variables that center around decisions the leader or group might make. Simply looking at the river in front of them is not enough. If they expand their perspective and organize their evaluation (of how or even if to cross the river) into objective and subjective factors, they may discover new, and perhaps better, options. By thinking in terms of objective and subjective factors, the group can make decisions that will minimize the accident potential.

For the sake of our example, let's say it is two o'clock in the afternoon, and the group has hiked seven miles this day already. It has also been raining for the past three days, but now the rain has ended and the weather seems to be clearing. The leaders knew they would have to cross this river, but they didn't anticipate it being this deep. The students have had classes and practice on crossing rivers. Some students are tired, but others are eager for the challenge. The water will be deeper than waist deep on the two shorter members of the group. There is a bridge 12 miles downstream (where a road crosses the river). A significant tributary joins the river two miles upstream, and the headwaters of the river are 15 miles upstream.

In this case, after discussing the situation with the students, the leaders decide to camp where they are, watch the water level, and see if it goes down overnight. They think this group can get across the river, but they want to give the tired students time to rest. They will re-evaluate and possibly attempt a crossing in the morning. If the river proves to be too much for the group, then they will hike up to the tributary and attempt to cross what should be two smaller rivers.

As this example illustrates, by looking beyond the immediate obstacle or hazard and carefully evaluating the big picture, the group may discover better options that allow members to more safely negotiate the hazard or obstacle.

Digging Deeper: Causes of Accidents

Hale's accident-potential diagram provides a broad framework for evaluating situations we may encounter in the outdoors. It is a convenient and useful way for leaders to approach a particular situation and make decisions about how to act.

Potentially Unsafe Conditions Due to:	**Potentially Unsafe Acts Due to:**	**Potential Errors in Judgment Due to:**
• Falling objects (rocks, etc)	• Inadequate protection	• Desire to please others
• Inadequate area security	• Inadequate instruction	• Trying to adhere to a schedule
• Weather	• Inadequate supervision	• Misperception
• Equipment/clothing	• Unsafe speed (fast/slow)	• New or unexpected situation
• Swift/cold water	• Inadequate food/drink	• Fatigue
• Animals/plants	• Poor position	• Distraction
• Physical or psychological profile of participants &/or staff	• Unauthorized/improper procedure	• Miscommunication
		• Disregarding instincts

Figure 1.3 *This chart identifies the principal causes of accidents in outdoor pursuits (Meyer and Williamson, 1979-2000). By listing the leading causes, accident investigators can examine the interplay of objective and subjective factors. Whereas Hale's work breaks factors into environmental and human, this matrix breaks subjective (human) factors into two separate categories.*

Dan Meyer and Jed Williamson (1979-2000) have developed a matrix that allows accident investigators to dig even deeper into the interplay of objective and subjective factors (see Figure 1.3). This matrix, originally developed in 1979, has evolved over time with a better understanding of the causes of accidents.

The Meyer/Williamson matrix is organized into three main categories of causes. As in the Hale matrix, there is a single category for objective factors; however, the subjective factors are split into two categories. Under each category are more specific, yet still broad, subcategories.

The Meyer/Williamson matrix, offering distinct points of inquiry, is useful for organizing an accident analysis. Each cause on the list helps the examiner ask certain questions to understand the specific details of the accident itself. For example, in one incident "unsafe speed" might mean someone descended a snow slope too fast and lost control. In another, it might mean that a climbing party ascended its route too slowly and was forced to do an unplanned bivouac on the side of the mountain.

Potentially Unsafe Conditions are the objective or environmental factors that contribute to accidents. Often the causes listed under this category describe what happened, such as the victim was hit by a falling rock or the victim died of exposure to the weather. While environmental hazards are significant and are often referred to as the cause of an accident, it is important to realize that environmental factors are only hazardous when we choose to place ourselves near them or put ourselves in a potentially harmful situation in relation to them. In other words, a river is simply a river. It only becomes a potentially unsafe condition once we decide we need to cross it.

An error in judgment can occur if we draw from incorrect past experiences or if we lack relevant experiences altogether.

Potentially Unsafe Acts identify subjective hazards that represent actions we take in relation to the conditions. Often these acts, when considered individually, may not seem to cause an accident. But a combination of seemingly insignificant acts may ultimately become a list of contributing causes of an accident.

When a potentially unsafe condition is encountered, such as a river that needs to be crossed by wading, all the causes under this category of potentially unsafe acts may come into play. What procedure is used to cross the river? How are the people protected when crossing? How much and what kind of instruction has been given? What are the relative heights and weights of the group members? How fast should the group cross? What position do you take when crossing the river? Are people tired and hungry or rested and refreshed before stepping into the water?

Potential Errors in Judgment are subjective hazards that represent the decisions we make that lead to the acts we take. Simon Priest elaborates on judgment in more detail in Chapter Two, defining judgment as "... drawing on past experiences to substitute for current uncertainties." An error in judgment can occur if we draw from incorrect past experiences or if we lack relevant experiences altogether. An error may also occur if we do not fully anticipate the uncertainties. Other factors that influence judgment include the emotional state of the leader or group, how well the group communicates, and how the group perceives its abilities.

The potential errors identified in this category are often difficult to perceive and predict in group members or ourselves. Well-trained and experienced leaders, however, are cognizant of these factors and can consciously think about if or how they might be influencing their decisions.

Application

Applying these analytical tools to real accidents can help us understand how to use them and increase our understanding of how an accident occurred.

Case Study #1

At 9:30 a.m. on the fifth day of a 10-day backcountry ski trip in Wyoming, a group of 11 students and two leaders set out to ski three miles to the base of Patterson Peak. They would break trail to what was to become their next campsite, and once there, they would mound snow for snow shelters. They planned to move into this camp the next day.

Willy, one of the leaders, was at the front of the group, and Dave, the other leader, was at the back of the line, about 15 to 20 minutes behind. During the morning, as they crossed some flat areas, Dave felt a collapse of the snow pack. He did not think it was indicative of overall instability in the snow, however, so he did not mention it to Willy.

About mid-morning, the group broke out onto a 20-degree NNE-facing open slope. They could see that it extended uphill about 100 feet to a tree band, and then gradually the slope angle increased. There were both small and large trees midway up the slope. Above the band of trees, and not immediately obvious to the leaders or anyone else in the group, the slope steepened for about 400 feet as it rose to a cliff band. Willy decided that neither the slope nor the snow pack was a danger. He made a gradual descending traverse across the slope to the valley bottom and the future camp location. The rest of the group followed, arriving about noon.

Willy and Dave discussed whether to return by the route they had come or break a different trail back to camp. Dave wanted to avoid crossing the same slope because he felt it would be difficult for students carrying full packs and pulling sleds when they moved camp the next day. There was also a slope along the route that Dave thought posed an avalanche danger, and this, along with the collapsing snow he felt earlier, made him want to establish a new route back. The two instructors had a terse conversation about which route to take, but they failed to reach a decision. For the next hour and a half, they busied themselves making snow shelters.

At about 1:40 p.m. a student (Steve) came to Willy and Dave complaining of pain in his feet. Willy inspected Steve's feet and decided that the group needed to head back to camp. Again, Willy and Dave discussed the route. Willy felt using the already broken trail would be more efficient, and would allow them to get Steve back to camp more quickly. Dave acquiesced.

Willy started out leading the group back on the existing trail, and Dave again brought up the rear. Willy re-emphasized to the group what to do in the event of an avalanche, including skiing downhill, struggling to stay close to the surface, and creating an air pocket. Though Willy recognized the area as a potential avalanche slope, he didn't think it was threatening. He didn't establish spotters or have the students ski across one at a time.

When Willy got across, he turned to watch the others. Suddenly he heard a sound (like a crack) from up slope, and looking up, he saw the avalanche. He yelled at the students in the slide path—five of them—to "ski down!" Steve was already out of the way. Denise easily skied out of the path. Frank and Molly skied downhill and to the side but were caught by the slide. Roger looked at the avalanche and then at Willy, then waved his arms and yelled. He did not attempt to ski out of the slide path, even though he was a capable skier. The slide caught Roger and carried him down slope. He was on the surface for 20 to 25 feet before being buried. Frank was buried to his chest and Molly was buried to her waist. Willy saw that Frank and Molly were not in imminent danger, and he focused his attention on Roger.

About five or six minutes after the slide had stopped, Willy located Roger by using an avalanche transceiver and quickly uncovered the student's face. Roger was buried about three to four feet under the surface. He was completely encased in snow and was not breathing. No air pocket had been created. There was no pulse. Rescue breathing was begun immediately, and chest compressions were started as soon as his chest could be uncovered. The CPR efforts were continued for two hours. Unfortunately, they were unsuccessful.

Late that night the instructors were able to contact the

managers of their organization and inform them of the accident. Roger's body was flown out by helicopter the next morning. The students and instructors skied out that day as well.

An autopsy cited the primary cause of death as suffocation. There is a possibility that Roger's history of cardiovascular disease, described in the autopsy report as moderately severe coronary arteriosclerosis, may have reduced his chances of survival.

Accident Analysis:
Avalanche, Three Students Caught, One Fatality

Potentially Unsafe Conditions: *falling objects (in this case snow, in the form of an avalanche), inadequate area security (not paying attention to the snow-pack history), and physical/psychological profile*
Potentially Unsafe Acts: *improper procedure and poor position*
Potential Errors in Judgment: *misperception, desire to please others, disregarding instinct, distraction, and miscommunication*

The avalanche path faced north-northeast with the starting zone at the base of a limestone cliff. The width of the avalanche was roughly 350 feet and ran down slope approximately 420 feet. The crown wall varied in thickness from one to four feet, suggesting that wind had redistributed snow in the starting zone. The bed-surface slope-angle ranged from 33 to 40 degrees with an alpha angle of 26 degrees. Roger was the 21st person to cross the slope that day.

The area, in this case the slope, was not secured because it was not considered a hazard. The leaders didn't recognize how the cliff band above them could affect the stability of the snow pack. They could have avoided the slope entirely and chosen a different route.

Though Roger was a capable skier he reportedly seemed to "freeze in place" when the avalanche began to slide. It is often difficult to predict with any certainty how someone will behave in a crisis, no matter how well we think they (or we) are taught. Roger's physical profile (his pre-existing history of cardiac disease) may have contributed to his death as well, although not to the accident itself.

Dave and Willy didn't accurately evaluate the stability of the snow pack or fully evaluate the hazard presented by the slope. They relied on their evaluation of the snow from the snow pits they had dug (in another location) the day before. However, transferring data from one slope on a different day to a new slope on a new day is not the proper procedure and is inadequate when evaluating a particular slope. They also ignored important signs. On the previous day they noticed two naturally occurring avalanches that had run on northeast-facing slopes. Dave did not fully realize the importance of the "whumping" sounds (the snow pack collapsing) he felt earlier in the day.

Position was also a contributing cause of this accident as Roger, Molly, and Frank were close together and all three were caught. The leader allowed the students to group up and get into an improper position. Willy took the time to re-emphasize the actions to take if there was an avalanche, yet he didn't take one simple, additional step and instruct them to cross one at a time.

Since the condition of the slope wasn't accurately assessed, Willy and Dave misperceived the danger. They failed to recognize some obvious signs. It was estimated in the post-accident investigation that the slope probably slid every 10 years. There were groups of small trees in the slide path next to mature trees. The mature trees had branches broken off on the up-hill sides. Neither instructor noticed how the slope steepened (to 40 degrees) above them as it rose into the cliff band.

Willy's desire to please the students (by not having them break a new trail back to camp and to take the easiest route) clearly affected his judgment. The condition of Steve's foot became a distraction, contributing to the miscommunication that already existed between Willy and Dave.

Dave and Willy's communication was poor and there was tension between them. Their differing evaluations of snow conditions and route choice earlier in the day were not adequately discussed. As a result, Dave's concern about snowpack stability and the possible avalanche slope were not effectively communicated to Willy. Though Dave also failed to fully recognize the avalanche potential of the slope, it appears he may have disregarded his own instincts about the snow pack.

This case study shows the interrelation of the contributing causes that led to the accident. It further demonstrates how a post-accident analysis usually reveals a step-by-step sequence that leads to an unexpected result. When each cause is viewed alone, it may often appear insignificant, but in combination with others, it can complete a sequence of seemingly unrelated events that results in an accident. If any one of the links of the causal sequence had been broken, the accident might not have happened.

A post-accident analysis usually reveals a step-by-step sequence that leads to an unexpected result. If any one of the links of the causal sequence had been broken, the accident might not have happened.

Accident prevention involves identifying and eliminating these causes before the chain of events is complete and an unintended outcome occurs. If we can define an event phase for an activity (such as flying, walking, boating, hiking, climbing, etc.), examine the interrelationship of all the causal factors within each event, and finally look at the decisions that were made, then we should be able to make conclusions about how and why the accident happened.

The following incident provides another example of this aspect of accident evaluation.

Case Study #2

The first half of the 25-day mountaineering course had been very demanding. Traversing the rugged Chilean mountains, the group had been bushwhacking for days and navigating through snowstorms with zero visibility. At the end of two weeks, they descended to receive a re-supply of food, rested for a few days, and then set off for a second traverse of the range, this time into glacial terrain.

The group was camped on a moraine, about 180 feet above the toe of a large unnamed glacier. It had taken five tough days of lowland bushwhacking to get to this point, and they were behind schedule. They had only eight days to attempt the arduous 12-mile-wide crossing. Completion of the intended route first required getting onto the ice, and there were only a few good choices available.

The next day the group discovered that descending to the glacier was more difficult than expected. Two routes looked feasible. One was a steep descent on ice that was covered by rock. The area showed signs of recent rockslides. The second option followed a descending line of large boulders along a vague ridge. The two instructors put on helmets and began to pick their way down this line of boulders while the students waited.

The route they preferred consisted of jagged and freshly broken granite blocks that indicated the instability of the boulder field. A few times the instructors felt rocks move or teeter under them. The route was possible, but this was a group of 20 people, equipped with large backpacks, and they were in an extremely remote place. The instructors were not eager to lead the students through the difficult terrain and decided to retreat.

The students were disappointed when told the news. They had worked hard for 18 days to get there. Most of these students had never set foot on a glacier before, and it was just a stone's throw away. No one, instructors included, wanted to turn around and walk back the way they had come. They sought student opinions, but in the end this was an instructor decision.

Nothing mandated that the class cross the glacier. The organization had a long history of allowing groups to change routes or schedules in order to avoid a hazard too forceful to be crossed safely. It would be OK to turn around. However, the students were excited and ambitious about moving forward. They were a capable group and had been rising to new challenges day after day on this demanding route. After further consideration, the instructors decided, for purely subjective (personal) reasons, to continue. Their plan was to coach and monitor the group closely, and pick each step of the route carefully. They believed they could manage the risks that day and again the next.

They successfully passed through the boulder field that morning, practiced glacier-travel techniques on the ice all afternoon, and scouted their route across it for the following day. Because no camping options existed on the glacier's toe, they returned to camp by using the same route. By this time, the group had safely completed 50 individual trips through the boulder field.

The next morning, they set out once again for the boulder field. Sixty feet into it, one of the students, Jeff, set a rock, larger than a washing machine, into motion. Recognizing the danger immediately, he leapt for the top of the boulder in front of him. His left foot was the last thing up, and he did not move it quite fast enough. The large rock came to rest against his foot, pinning it against the rock on which he was now perched. A portion of the rock's weight (as well as a second smaller one) was now bearing on Jeff's boot. The pressure on his foot was tremendous.

The instructors positioned and drove into place wedge-shaped chock stones on either side of Jeff's leg to stabilize the mobile rocks and prevent the gap from tightening. A student, who was an EMT, addressed first aid needs. All other students were moved to a safe location and the accident scene was stabilized. All unnecessary motion in the boulder field was banned.

Moving the big rocks appeared nearly impossible and unnecessarily dangerous. With limited access down between the boulders, they worked quickly to dismantle Jeff's ankle gaiter, cut his laces, and work his boot open. Work was difficult and dangerous in the narrow gap between the big leaning rocks. They cut open the back panel of his boot (down to the sole), and cut the inner boot similarly along the Achilles tendon. Nothing would budge. They cut the whole back of his boot into purple plastic shards. They cut open both of his socks, down the calf to the heel, and sliced his pant leg. This time, pulling hard under Jeff's direction, the foot slowly came free. About a half-hour had passed.

Jeff's foot was misshapen, with a sock-fabric pattern deeply imprinted and with his toes and lower foot a deep blue. Distal circulation and sensation were non-existent, but as the minutes passed they began to return. Even the twisted shape of his foot began to remold itself—until it started swelling like a balloon. His foot had indeed been squished by the weight of the rock, but thankfully the tons of granite came to rest against the rigid sole of his plastic boot. The injury was bad, but it could have been a whole lot worse.

It was a long evacuation: five days of effort and two days waiting for a swollen river to subside before it was all over. Jeff crawled, hobbled on makeshift crutches, and was carried. Luckily, his foot eventually healed.

Accident Analysis:
Foot Entrapment in a Boulder Field

Potentially Unsafe Conditions: *falling objects (rocks)*
Potentially Unsafe Acts: *unauthorized or improper procedure, poor position*
Potential Errors in Judgment: *desire to please others, trying to adhere to a schedule*

The lead instructor on this account is a competent mountaineer and talented educator. None of his decisions were made lightly or without careful consideration. This incident and the events leading up to it illustrate what instructors must do every day; i.e., balance student education and experience while managing risk.

Nevertheless, the instructor still wonders if he asked for this accident. It was a goal-oriented course with a steep learning curve for each of the students. They were having an incredible experience as they forged through new country. The instructor's desire to see this experience continue for the students contributed to the decision to descend the boulder field.

It is important to take the analysis of this incident further. There were some important factors at work here. There are really two incidents in this story; 1) the decision to negotiate the boulder field and 2) the response and effort once Jeff's foot became stuck. It is the former that deserves greater analysis while recognizing that the effort to free Jeff's foot was handled well and with great effort and tenacity.

Because of all the group had been through and accomplished prior to the accident, there may have been a sense of invincibility among the students and instructors. Because they were behind schedule and had endured so much to get to the glacier, the need (real or perceived) to stick to a schedule was an influential factor. It is also clear that there was a desire to please others (the students). All of these factors influenced the group's decision to go into the boulder field.

Sometimes circumstances draw us into accepting higher levels of risk than usual. We must ask ourselves: does the educational experience justify the risk? This story clearly illustrates how important the subjective factors are when evaluating hazards. We all wish to have great outcomes for our students, but at what cost? The success of a course should not be measured solely by whether or not a route is completed.

The instructors were familiar with and experienced in this type of terrain and felt the boulder field was within the group's ability. As we pointed out, the boulder field had been successfully negotiated four times, equaling 50 individual trips, before Jeff's foot became trapped between the rocks.

The hazard of loose and rolling rock is significant and one which must always be anticipated in the mountains. The instructor and the students felt they were unlucky in this incident, but perhaps luck played a more positive role than they realized. It may have been good luck that Jeff was wearing plastic boots and the rocks happened to catch him at the rigid sole. Had he been a little slower in moving out of the way, had the rock rolled at a slightly different angle, or had the rocks been shaped differently, the situation could have been much worse.

Collecting Accident Data

A determination of cause, arrived at through consistently applied analytical methods and by using standardized terminology, helps accident investigators create a statistical database for analysis, observation of trends, and prediction of future problem areas. It is our intention that the accounts of actual accidents presented here illustrate the usefulness of this information exchange. The number of times someone has had his or her foot caught between two massive boulders is low, but the number of incidents of students incorrectly fastening their climbing harnesses or falling during a river crossing are much higher. As our examples show, one rare event resulted in a significant injury while more common events fortunately did not.

A review of accident data presented by the American and

PRIMARY CAUSES	CONTRIBUTING CAUSES
Fall or slip on rock	Climbing unroped
Slip on snow or ice	Exceeding abilities
Falling rock or object	Inadequate equipment
Exceeding abilities	Weather
Avalanche	No/inadequate protection
Exposure	Climbing alone
Illness	No hard hat
Stranded	Nut/chock pulled out
Rappel failure/error	Darkness
Loss of control/glissade	Piton pulled out
Fall into crevasse/moat	Party separated
Failure to follow route	Poor position
Piton pulled out	Failure to test holds
Nut/chock pulled out	Exposure
Faulty use of crampons	Inadequate belay
Lightning	Failure to follow directions
Skiing	Illness
Ascending too fast	Equipment failure
Equipment failure	Other
Other	
Unknown	

Figure 1.4 *Primary and contributing causes of climbing accidents, from* Accidents in North American Mountaineering. *The items are listed according to frequency of occurrence.*

Canadian alpine clubs in the annual summary of *Accidents in North American Mountaineering* includes a listing of primary as well as contributing causes in climbing accidents. For the sake of our discussion, we will presume that the accidents in these cases resulted in injuries. Fifty-nine percent of the accidents occurred on ascent, 36 percent on descent, and five percent were unknown. Figure 1.4 is extrapolated from the presentation of data. The lists are compiled from most frequent to least frequent causes. Note that each list is independent of the other.

It is more difficult to find accident data specific to outdoor adventure programs. There is no central reporting agency, nor is there a mandate for programs to report the data. In an effort to change this situation, the Wilderness Risk Managers' Committee initiated a voluntary incident reporting project in 1991. Contributions have been meager, however, mainly due to a lack of incentive to report and a hesitancy to make this data public (even though identities would be held in confidence). In 1999, the Association for Experiential Education (AEE), which provides accreditation for adventure programs, began requiring accredited programs to submit data. This incentive should strengthen efforts to establish a representative database for adventure programs.

In one study that does exist, AEE compiled available data from 18 adventure programs (Leemon, 1998). The 1998 report contains findings consistent with those presented in *Accidents in North American Mountaineering*. Both reports identify the leading (primary) cause of injuries as falls or slips.

Two other organizations, the National Outdoor Leadership School (NOLS) and Outward Bound (OB), have come up with similar findings. NOLS has maintained a database of accidents since 1984. Figure 1.5 provides an overview of the injury data over a four-year period, and fall/slip is listed as the primary cause. OB also keeps a record of accidents that occur during their programs. According to Lewis Glenn, Vice President of Safety and Program for Outward Bound USA,

Injury Type (Top Ten)	#	%
Athletic	365	51%
Soft tissue	171	24%
Dental	31	4%
Immersion foot	27	4%
Burn	23	3%
Dislocation	23	3%
Fracture	20	3%
Other	16	2%
Blister	14	2%
Head	10	1%
	700	97%

Injury Cause (Top Ten)	#	%
Fall/slip	203	29%
Overuse	175	25%
Previous history	56	8%
Failed to follow instructions	37	5%
Carelessness	37	5%
Animal/insect/plant	23	3%
Poor position	13	2%
Stove fire/spilled hot water	12	4%
Exceeded ability	12	2%
Equipment	11	1%
	577	81%

Activity at Time of Injury	#	%
Hiking w/pack	292	41%
In camp	131	18%
Mountaineering	34	5%
Rock climbing	29	4%
Hiking without a pack	30	4%
River kayak/raft/canoe	30	4%
Sea kayaking	27	4%
Skiing	28	4%
Cooking	26	4%
Horse	9	1%
	636	90%

Figure 1.5 *This chart provides an injury profile for the National Outdoor Leadership School (NOLS). It identifies the top-10 most common injuries suffered during a NOLS course during a four-year period, from September 1, 1994, to August 31, 1998. The data includes 710 total injury incidents, 346 of which resulted in evacuation from the field.*

falls or slips is the leading cause of injury within their organization as well.

It is interesting to note that in all four sets of data, one representing the general public and three representing adventure programs, falls/slips ws noted as the leading cause of accidents and/or injuries. The types of falls reported in *Accidents in North American Mountaineering* reflect climbing-related incidents specifically while the AEE, NOLS and OB data includes many less-spectacular accidents (such as falls on a trail while backpacking or falls in camp).

Near miss incidents are often predictors of future accidents.

Near Misses

Accidents that result in injury or death often receive the greatest amount of attention, both within an organization and from the media. Another type of incident, however, that may not receive adequate attention but should nevertheless be monitored closely is the near miss. The story of the Clearwater River crossing at the beginning of this chapter was used to illustrate this type of incident. A near miss (or close call) is a potentially dangerous situation where safety is compromised but no injury occurs. Like an accident, it is an unplanned and unforeseen event. This rules out routine top-rope falls, failure to roll a kayak for a beginning student, or a fall on the trail with no injury. It is a situation where those involved express relief when the incident ended without harm.

Near miss incidents are often predictors of future accidents. Haddock (1999) researched studies of industrial accidents where it was found "that for each serious injury or fatality, there were 10 minor injuries, 30 cases of property damage, and 600 incidents with no visible injury or damage."

NOLS records near miss incidents in a separate database and uses the information to look for trends. As is the case with injuries, we see falls/slips as a leading cause of near misses (shown in Figure 1.6).

The importance of collecting data on accidents, incidents, and near misses becomes clear when we understand the "High Reliability Theory" of accidents (Sagan, 1993). This theory proposes that safety can be achieved through the implementation of appropriate organizational design and

Near Miss Cause List (Top Ten)	#	%
Fall/slip	73	24%
Rockfall	40	13%
Failed to follow instructions	33	11%
Lost	16	5%
Exceeded ability	13	4%
Loose rock (not rockfall)	11	4%
Weather	11	4%
Stove/fire/spilled hot water	10	3%
Animal/insect/plant	10	3%
Carelessness	8	3%
	225	**73%**

Activity at Time of Near Miss (Top Ten)	#	%
Hiking with a pack	69	25%
Mountaineering/glacier/snow climb	59	21%
Rock climbing	36	13%
In camp	27	10%
River kayak/raft/canoe	20	7%
Hiking without a pack	17	6%
River crossing	16	6%
Small group expeditions	13	5%
Cooking	12	4%
Sea kayaking	10	4%
	279	**91%**

Figure 1.6 *This chart lists the top-10 causes of near-miss incidents that occurred during NOLS courses over a four-year span, from September 1, 1994, to August 31, 1998. Of the 307 total near-miss incidents, the most common cause (slips and falls) mirrors the most common cause of accidents (in NOLS courses) during the same time frame.*

management techniques. Sagan listed four components of high-reliability organizations:

1) Leadership Safety Objectives
2) The Need for Redundancy
3) Decentralization, Culture, and Continuity, and
4) Organizational Learning.

Leadership Safety Objectives simply means that an organization's management and leadership establish safety priorities and emphasize these priorities regularly. By admitting that people can make mistakes and systems can fail, high reliability organizations also accept the *Need for Redundancy*, and build back-ups or redundancy into their operations. In an outdoor adventure context, redundancy might include such things as using multiple instructors per group; making sure each instructor has at least a minimum level of medical training; and creating pre-planned emergency procedures covering both the field and support aspects of an operation.

Decentralization, Culture, and Continuity, in an industrial context, means that anyone on the assembly line can stop production when there is a safety concern. In the outdoor adventure context, it means that leaders can exercise their judgments and make decisions appropriate to the situation at hand. High reliability organizations also have a pervasive "culture of safety" throughout the organization. Each employee embraces the organization's safety priorities and applies them to his or her areas. High reliability organizations also rely on continuity and consistency in their staff trainings.

The fourth component, *Organizational Learning*, means that the organization learns from its experiences and mistakes. This is the aspect of the theory that is most relevant to our discussion in this chapter. The analysis of accidents, including near-miss incidents, can greatly enhance organizational learning by means of trial and error. As the data is analyzed, it often reveals patterns, which in turn suggest improvements an organization can make in its programming and practices. By studying its own mistakes (and the mistakes of others), an organization with a strong desire to learn can adjust its routines and activities over time to achieve greater effectiveness and a higher degree of reliability. By reporting near misses and seemingly insignificant incidents, that organization can help others learn as well.

In contrast, the Normal Accident Theory (Perrow, 1984) suggests that in complex systems risk factors can be linked in multiple and unpredictable ways. This, in turn, can create interactive complexity that can defy organizational management. The failure of one part may coincide with the failure of a different (and possibly unexpected) part. Components of a system can be "tightly coupled" (that is, the parts are closely related), or "loosely coupled" (the parts are not directly related). For instance, if we look back at the avalanche case study, Steve's sore foot was a loosely coupled component of the accident while the "whomping" sound that Dave heard in the snow pack is a more tightly coupled component. Both were factors in the accident, but having sore feet certainly doesn't cause people to die in avalanches. When little flexibility is possible, or when there are few opportunities for a person to intervene or "contain" the components of an event, a cascade of failures can advance out of control and lead to a major accident. On a basic level, Perrow's theory is that these system characteristics produce normal or system accidents and that these accidents are inevitable.

Adventure programs are uniquely complex. We pursue adventures with inherent risks that may have tragic consequences, and we rely on systems that are both technical (as in ropes and anchors), and behavioral (as in judgment, decision-making, and the ability to perform without error). In our situations, the risk factors can be both loosely and tightly coupled. As a result, the potential for small accidents to cascade into significant accidents is great.

The High Reliability Theory suggests an organization can learn from its mistakes, but Perrow's Normal Accident Theory suggests otherwise. Instead, Perrow's theory suggests that the politics of an organization will even interfere with the analysis of an accident. The credit for success or the blame for mistakes must be given to or placed on individual people within the organization. As the organization attempts to protect itself, the possibility of learning is obscured. In this type of environment, the prevalence of faulty reporting of accidents is more likely. The incentives to cover up accidents or under-report events are strong, particularly among workers at the field level. No one wants to be blamed. Everyone wants to have a good safety record.

We can accept Perrow's premise and still consciously choose to avoid feeling the need to blame someone. However, the High Reliability Theory offers the better model, and organizational learning should be embraced. The lessons learned from the study of accidents, while not a substitute for actual experience, can be very useful to outdoor leaders when they are faced with similar situations. The discussion, analysis, and evaluation of accidents are important and necessary tools for outdoor leaders to use if they are to learn how to reduce accidents.

To Share or Not to Share

There is always a concern that legal action might be brought against an organization following a serious accident. This concern needs to be considered in an organization's response to the incident. What the response will be and whether or not information will be openly shared depends on the specific circumstances of the situation. The organization has an obligation to protect itself (including staff, participants and trustees) from criminal or civil claims. The financial stability of the organization, too, needs to be protected. However, the organization needs to consider how it wants to be perceived by the affected parties and the public. (This issue is addressed more thoroughly at the end of Chapter Four.)

It has been shown in some cases that sharing information early and being empathetic to the families of victims can result in a positive relationship where legal issues are resolved quickly and fairly. Additionally, today's information-saturated society expects and often demands disclosure of information regarding accidents. It often boils down to not if, but how information about an accident is disseminated. Anticipating these situations and developing a plan that guides the organization in how it will disseminate accident information is strongly advised. At some point in the process, though, the legal concerns will be resolved, and at that time (at least), the accident can be used as a learning tool.

The fear of admitting possible mistakes and exposing the program to possible legal action inhibits outdoor leaders and our profession from improving.

When politics interfere with organizational learning we lose out on valuable lessons. The fear of admitting possible mistakes and exposing the program to possible legal action inhibits outdoor leaders and our profession from improving. It is only through careful examination and the open sharing of information that we can learn from our experiences and advance the potential that future accidents can be prevented. We should always focus on saving lives rather than saving jobs.

The Human Factor

The human factor is the most difficult to accurately document in any sequence of events, but it is usually the most important to understand. Most people in the field of risk management or accident investigation will agree that the human element comprises the largest portion of an accident equation.

Human beings have always made errors, and they always will. Acceptance of that idea is the foundation upon which all analysis of human error and the factors that induce human error rests. Perfect human performance in all situations is simply impossible. What works brilliantly in one set of circumstances may be quite imperfect in another, as the origins of the error can be quite different.

Systemic human failures may also have a place in the causal chain. An accident inquiry should always include an examination of human errors produced or induced by the use or misuse of a particular design of equipment. One person's decisions and actions should be considered against the reasonable degree of performance that could be expected from another person with equivalent knowledge, qualifications, and experience. Consideration must not be given to the human failure alone, but one should also examine why the failure occurred in the first place.

Some researchers differentiate between task errors (i.e., unsafe acts) and decision errors; others maintain that there is no real difference, they are all just people errors. If we understand the information available to people, the goals they are pursuing, and the level of their experience, we will stop blaming people for making decision errors. This does not mean we should stop looking at poor outcomes. In fact, the reverse is true. But the critical difference is that the discovery of an error should be the beginning of the inquiry rather than the end. The real work is to find out the complete range of factors that resulted in the undesirable outcome.

One natural outcome that should be resisted is our tendency to place blame and give in to public pressure that "something" must be done immediately. An accident, particularly one with serious injuries or fatalities, is highly visible for a time. People close to an accident investigation are often amazed to watch the media coverage of the event. Within hours, it seems, various experts are brought on TV to speculate about possible causes, and questionable scenarios are analyzed through an extreme range of possibilities, most of which bear little resemblance to the facts of the event. The pressure to act immediately is all too often based on preliminary speculation and incomplete information and can lead to an over-reactive response with demands for more rules, regulations, and restrictions that ultimately may be unnecessary or redundant.

It is only through a careful and comprehensive investigation that the most probable causal sequence is discovered. And even then, although some accident causes can be proven without question, many others are the result of highly educated guesses or conclusions.

Yes, humans are all capable of committing unsafe acts. But we are capable of learning from them as well. Errors, in particular, are an essential part of the process of learning. Divorced from the legal arena that often inhibits our ability to learn from mistakes, accidents provide the catalyst for improvement. Consequently, accident analysis has contributed to safer programming and no doubt prevented a great number of injuries as a result.

Effective Outdoor Leadership

By Simon Priest © 2000

This chapter examines the theory and practice of outdoor leadership and its two most critical components: safety and judgment. The concepts of leadership and judgment are defined, explained conceptually, and discussed specifically in relation to outdoor adventures. The author also offers methods for improving judgment and provides examples of factors that can affect the decision-making process.

The group was ascending the glacier more slowly than they had hoped, and some of the students were noticeably fatigued. Although they had already spent 10 hours hiking and climbing, they still had at least three hours to go before they reached their intended destination: an alpine hut overlooking the river of ice. They would need to negotiate snow-covered crevasses to reach the shelter, and in their tired condition the possibility of making a mistake and having an accident was greater than if they waited to proceed till morning.

Although the instructors were not looking forward to continuing, there were also costs associated with stopping for the night. The group would need to spend an hour probing the glacier for a safe area and digging tent sites. Further, it would take considerable time to break down camp and rope up for travel in the morning. As a result, it seemed likely the students would not reach the hut until lunchtime. Camping now meant that the group would lose almost an entire day of crevasse-rescue training.

The alpine hut they were headed for was situated on a rocky knoll. The area was dotted with wildflowers, and the views were stunning. From there, the group would be set up to spend two days practicing mountaineering and glacier-travel skills. They would have access to a shelter—conducive to comfortable classroom time and evening meals—along with campsites and water. Further, the location was ideal for easy access on and off the ice; from camp it was only a 20-minute hike to a perfect crevasse-rescue site. Consequently, students would be able to leave much of their equipment at camp and could travel with light loads. The group was definitely looking forward to reaching its objective. To some, stopping for the night would be a disappointment—to others a failure.

Several of the students were eager to continue, and many said they'd be willing to take weight from their tired fellow climbers. The leaders were forced to make a difficult choice. Stopping might lead to dissension among group members, but it would also result in a rested group that could travel more safely through the crevasse field. Yet the group believed it could make the hut, even if it meant a long night. The instructors had to weigh all these factors before making a final decision.

Leadership is a process of influence. People who become outdoor leaders influence group members to create, identify, work toward, achieve, and share mutually acceptable goals. With informal group settings, more than one group member can emerge to fulfill various leadership roles. In formal settings, however, the outdoor leader is typically designated by a sponsoring agency as being "in charge." Also, it is generally understood that designated outdoor leaders hold legal and moral responsibility for the learning, supervision, and safety of their groups, as well as for protecting the natural environment (Priest & Gass, 1998).

In the introductory scenario, the group's leaders were responsible for the students' learning and well-being. Although most people reasonably expect this from an instructor, it is not always clear what is best in a given situation. In this case, the leaders had to weigh several factors before making a decision: Stopping for the night would not have been ideal, but it would have been prudent. On the other hand, the hut provided a more comfortable setting with greater opportunity for practicing the crevasse-rescue techniques they were hoping to learn. Most of the students wanted to continue. The instructor wanted to please the group and knew that going against their wishes could lead to a drop in morale.

Which alternative the instructors ultimately selected is not obvious in the scenario nor are similarly difficult decisions obvious in real-life endeavors. Often the choice depends on an instructor and his skill level, experiences, and judgment. One of the most important questions an organization must ask, therefore, is *what does it take to be a good leader?* Are there skills, characteristics, or experiences that best qualify someone to lead others in the outdoors? And if the traits can be identified, what can an instructor or organization do to improve or enhance these qualities?

This chapter examines some of the key competencies that are critical to the success of the outdoor leader. It also includes a process for analyzing dangers that instructors can use to minimize the potential for an accident. And finally, the chapter offers suggestions for developing and improving judgment, that all-important quality that is often considered the essential trait in an instructor. Although this information can in no way guarantee that an accident will not happen, together these concepts can be used to reduce the potential by examining what it means and what it takes to be an effective outdoor leader.

The Increasing Need for Outdoor Leaders

Outdoor leaders have never been more in demand. In brief, the past 20 years have seen an exponential growth in the number of people seeking their leisure experiences outdoors. With the increase has come a growing number of outdoor accidents (damage to the users) and an increase in environmental impact (damage to the resources). Perhaps this has occurred because of the common public attitude that encourages competing against, conquering, and dominating nature. In any competition, however, there is a loser. Either the users lose (when they suffer an injury) or the natural resources lose (when they are damaged or destroyed). In any case, effective leadership is necessary to prevent both kinds of damage and to ensure that the user and the resources co-exist in harmony. Given that modern trends point toward further growth (KPMG Peat Marwick, 1997), the need to prepare more effective outdoor leaders is obvious. But what is the formula for success?

During the 1980s, several well-noted research studies attempted to identify the key competencies that are critical to the success of an outdoor leader (Green, 1981; Swiderski, 1981; Buell, 1981; Priest, 1984; Raiola, 1986; and Priest, 1986). Two competencies, safety and judgment, showed up in the top-10 lists of most studies, and in some studies they were identified as *the* most important competencies for a leader to possess. These two skills will be discussed in detail later in this chapter, but first we will examine the leadership traits revealed by a meta-analysis of these studies (Priest, 1987).

Leadership Skills: Hard, Soft, and Meta

Effective outdoor leadership is a subtle combination of factors that includes hard, soft, and "meta" skills. *Hard skills* include technical, safety, and environmental skills, the kind of solid and tangible competencies that can usually be measured through ratings or certifications. *Soft skills*, such as the ability to organize, teach, and facilitate group interactions, are a little less tangible, and more difficult to assess. They are also more difficult to learn and hone. *Meta skills* are higher-order core abilities, such as problem-solving and decision-making, that enhance the hard and soft skills. Meta skills "glue" the first two categories together, integrating them in a workable systemic manner and allowing the outdoor leader to become fully effective.

Hard Skills

Hard skills are usually prerequisites for hiring and are often offered as part of an instructor-training program. The skills are measurable in nature, and a certification of completion may be offered to show that an appropriate level of competency has been reached. The three subcategories of hard skills include technical, safety, and environmental.

Technical skills refer to competencies specific to the

Hard Skills	Soft Skills	Meta Skills
Technical skills Safety skills Environmental skills	Organizational skills Instructional skills Facilitation skills	Flexible leadership style Experienced-based judgment Problem-solving skills Decision-making skills Effective communication Professional ethics

actual adventure activities or outdoor pursuits being led. Two examples of technical skills are the ability to climb at a certain level and the ability to paddle a particular grade or class of whitewater. In order to maintain group control during these activities, outdoor leaders must be able to perform at a proficiency higher than that of the group members, thus giving them a safety margin or "cushion of competence."

While technical skills are specific to a particular activity, *safety skills* are necessary to enjoy nearly any adventure activity in a sound and prudent manner. These competencies include skills that may help prevent accidents as well as those that may be needed in the event of an emergency. Examples of safety skills include navigation, survival, weather interpretation, hypothermia prevention, first aid, accident response, and search and rescue.

Given the enormous number of people who seek adventure in the outdoors and the trend toward further growth, an organization cannot afford to travel and camp with environmentally damaging impact. Consequently, *environmental skills* are competencies that an outdoor leader needs in order to prevent harm to the natural surroundings. This includes encouraging minimum-impact travel, practicing Leave-No-Trace camping techniques, and role modeling good behaviors (such as carrying out the garbage and not cross-cutting switchback trails).

Soft Skills

Soft skills help ensure a smooth delivery of course material and help provide a quality experience. Examples of soft skills include the ability to plan and prepare for an outing, incorporate sequential learning into a course, use different teaching styles, create an atmosphere of trust and cooperation, and resolve conflicts as they arise. The three subcategories of soft skills are organizational skills, instructional skills, and facilitation skills.

A well-planned trip has a higher likelihood of safety and success than its counterpart. *Organizational skills* permit a leader to prepare, execute, and evaluate experiences for the specific needs of each particular client or student group. For example, an outdoor leader may be expected to arrange transportation, food, and lodging for participants. She may also need to schedule activities, select routes, and plan contingencies, or secure the necessary permits, equipment, and clothing to make the experience a success.

Without *instructional skills* an instructor can't effectively teach students the skills specific to the activity, the environment, or to student and group safety. Teaching skiing in a series of progressions, for instance, helps prepare students for more advanced techniques later in a course. Effective use of teaching aids is another example of an important instructional skill.

Facilitation skills are those that foster productive group dynamics, allowing students to develop relationships while they work toward completing specific tasks. Outdoor leaders need to communicate effectively, foster personal trust and group cooperation, and even resolve conflicts on occasion. They also need to know how to brief and debrief a group, and guide students in reflecting on their experiences once an adventure is over. Sometimes it is in reflection that the greatest learning takes place.

Meta Skills

Meta skills cement the hard and soft skills together. They include an instructor's ability to make decisions based on experience and judgment. They also include a leader's ability to recognize and examine multiple options, and make well-thought-out choices. The subcategories of meta skills include the following: flexible leadership style, experience-based judgment, problem-solving skills, decision-making ability, effective communication, and professional ethics.

There's more than one way to use your influence as group leader. *Flexible leadership style* means knowing how, why, and when to use differing leadership methods. For instance, under many conditions the decision-making process of a group can be democratic or shared. That means the students have a say in determining thc group's choices. In many programs, the leader is free to be abdicratic; i.e., to abdicate or delegate responsibility to the group. An example of this might be a program that includes a student-led expedition at the end of the course. With little direct input from the instructor, students are allowed to make decisions that will directly affect the end result.

At times, however, a leader must be autocratic; giving orders and expecting them to be carried out. Although the autocratic leadership style might seem most appropriate in an emergency, there are less obvious situations that might call for the same tactic as well. For instance, although the students in our introductory scenario may have wanted to continue, and while their input was worthwhile, the instructors were responsible for making the final decision regarding whether to camp or continue. Ultimately, an instructor must have the ability to adapt his leadership style and adopt the one that best suits the circumstances.

Experience-based judgment is required when leaders confront situations where pertinent information is unknown, missing, or vague.

Experience-based judgment is required when leaders confront situations where pertinent information is unknown, missing, or vague. If we remember that an adventure is defined by the presence of an uncertain outcome, it seems critical that outdoor leaders be skilled in this area. By considering past experiences and utilizing sound judgment, outdoor leaders can appropriately substitute educated guesses for unknown or ambiguous information.

Again, the chapter's lead story can help clarify this point. In the scenario, the instructors were in the best position to use experience-based judgment to help make a final decision as to whether they should camp or continue. They were also in the best position to know what the snowbridges might be like that evening versus the next morning, and what type of performance they could expect from the fatigued students. Because they had dealt with similar situations or conditions on past trips, they could draw on their experiences in order to fill in some of the unknowns.

Experience-based judgment becomes extremely important when the act of delaying a decision might further compound a problem. An inexperienced instructor, for instance, might hesitate when deciding where to cross a river in the hope that additional time and observation would also provide additional clues. Although the map and written venue guide clearly note that there are two known and used crossing sites, the leader, not satisfied with either, sends a group to scout for alternatives. In the meantime, if the weather deteriorates, matters would only become worse; students would become preoccupied with staying warm and comfortable while the river continues to rise.

Sound judgment comes from surviving past judgment calls (good or bad), analyzing those successes and failures, and applying what has been learned to future situations. In turn, this requires that outdoor leaders gain plenty of intensive and extensive field experience. Accumulation of experiences by itself does not ensure sound judgment; lack of experience, however, cannot possibly provide the critical foundation necessary for the interpolation or extrapolation of uncertain information.

Problem-solving skills help leaders identify and solve both simple and complex dilemmas. Simple problems may appear straightforward, but if they are not handled correctly, they can rapidly escalate into something much worse. Consider, for example, the instructor who provides a quick fix to a student's pack by using cord or tape to secure a broken buckle. Later, because the student cannot easily remove or adjust the "fixed" pack, she may develop impressive and disabling hip blisters.

Sometimes an instructor may need to be creative, and other times an analytical approach might be best. Often a combination of both provides the most appropriate solution. Analytical skills might be used, for example, when the leader needs to recognize a problem, define the crux, anticipate the outcome, and identify several possible solutions. Using this information, she must then be able to select the most probable solution, put it into action, and evaluate its effectiveness.

If the problem-solving effort temporarily stalls, creative techniques are often useful to get things going again. Creative techniques include brainstorming (an open expression of ideas with no fear of criticism), extended effort (encouraging group members not to give up too quickly on an idea), attribute listing (making an inventory), forced relationships (comparing and contrasting ideas with the hope of creating new from old), and deferred prejudice (remaining open to new ideas; i.e. thinking out of the box).

Decision-making skills enable leaders to select the most desirable option from an assortment of alternatives. This includes being capable of diverging (or building up a range of several options) and then converging (or narrowing down the range to pick one best one). In the introductory scenario, the group initially identified only two options: make camp on the glacier or continue on to the hut. In order to build up its range of options, the group could have considered taking a long break (in order to cook dinner and perhaps even take a short nap) before proceeding. Maybe they could have taken an alternative (and safer) route across the ice. Another option would have been for the group to split (with one team staying and the second, stronger team moving on). Or they could have decided to retrace their route and call off the trip altogether. Typically, the wider the range of options created through divergence, the better.

Convergence, or narrowing the realm of possibilities to one, is generally the most difficult part of the decision-making process. The following methods can be used to effectively evaluate and narrow one's choices: gathering (collecting all pertinent information), weeding out (removing inappropriate options), organizing (ranking the remaining options), weighting (considering the positive, negative, and neutral aspects of each option), and choosing (selecting a path or preferred option).

Before making a final decision, the leaders in the opening scene should have gathered all pertinent information, including factors like the weather, time of day, and snow conditions, along with the group's experience level, hunger, and fatigue. Next, they could have examined their options, noting the costs and benefits of each. During this process, some options might have been immediately discarded as inappropriate. Once the options were organized and weighed, the weaker alternatives could easily be eliminated. Ultimately a final choice could have been made. By building up ideas and then narrowing the range, the leaders would have used a sound approach to decision-making.

Effective communication is a process of information exchange between two or more people that results in a desired behavioral change. A message (in the form of ideas, actions, or emotions) is transmitted along a pathway of audio, visual, and tactile channels. When this process is incomplete or ineffective, poor communication is the result. For instance, when an instructor tells students in the front of the group to take a break "up the trail, around the corner," he should not be surprised when he arrives at "the corner" only to find no students. An unclear exchange like this will often lead to confusion and frustration.

Experience, coupled with reflection, is the foundation of good judgment.

Outdoor leaders need to be able to send and receive messages not only through verbal means, but through nonverbal ones as well. They should be able to generate, transmit, receive, and decode messages on an ongoing basis, and they must be able to interpret whether or not messages that have been sent were received. Leaders also need to be able to use paraphrasing and impression checking in order to confirm that the message received was indeed the same as the message sent.

As with most disciplines, certain professional actions are more appropriate than others. *Professional ethics* refer to the moral standards and value systems that outdoor leaders have and adventure education demands. Challenge by choice, for example, is an ethic that defines adventure programming. Its message is that people have the right to choose their level of participation in activities and should not be coerced into doing something they are unwilling to do.

Similarly, outdoor leaders hold enormous power over their students, and certain ethics guide leaders away from possible abuses of this power, such as deception, secrecy, or sexual contact with participants. As a result, ethical decision-making should be a concern for all outdoor leaders.

Cumulatively, these dozen competency areas make up the effective outdoor leader. We can visualize them as working together to create a kind of brick wall of skills (see Figure 2.1). At the foundation is an overall understanding of outdoor and adventure education, with particular emphasis on its psychology, history, and philosophy. The wall is built by layering the soft skills on top of the hard skills. The meta skills, like mortar, bind the hard and soft skills together, increasing the strength and endurance of the whole structure.

It is clear that the most effective outdoor leaders are skilled in all three competency areas. However, there is ongoing debate over how to best prepare our future leaders. Although the ingredients may be known, the exact combination of skills needed to create the most effective leader remains elusive. What is clear is that experience will continue to play a primary role. Experience, coupled with reflection, is the foundation of good judgment. Well-rounded leaders have experience in a wide range of settings, with a wide variety of students. They have tested their hard, soft, and meta skills in a broad cross-section of many situations. Consequently, the combination of their experiences improves the overall quality of their adventure programs.

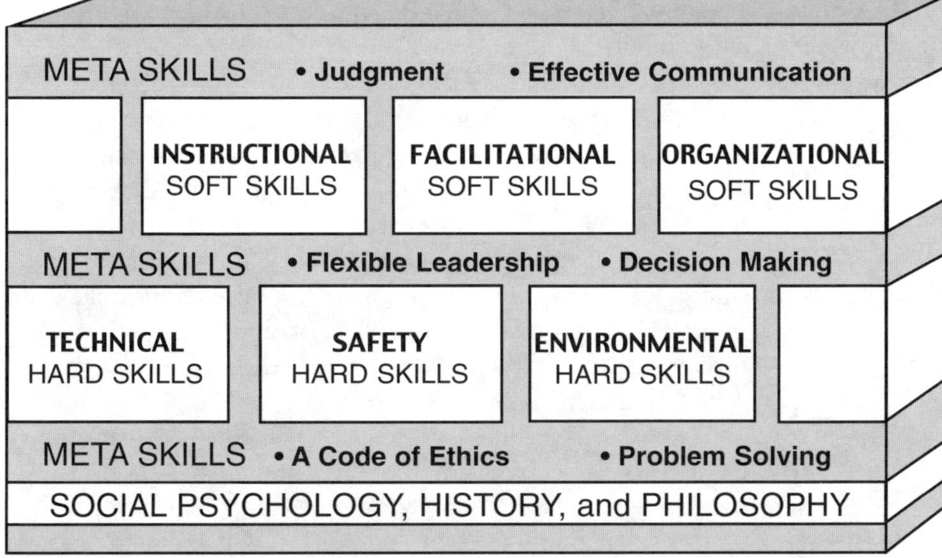

Figure 2.1 *This illustration provides a visual metaphor for leadership skills. Like a brick wall, hard, soft, and meta skills combine to create a solid and lasting framework for the outdoor leader. (Adapted from Priest's 1997 work.)*

The "Accident Potential"

Risk management refers to the collective actions that an outdoor leader or organization might take before, during, and after an outing in order to reduce the potential for an accident and in order to minimize the potential for injury or loss.

An *accident* is any undesired or unexpected event that results in an injury or loss. *Losses* can be physical (broken bones, sprained joints, death), social (embarrassment in front of one's peers), emotional (fear), or financial (not getting your money's worth). *Risk* is the likelihood that these valuable losses will occur, and is a measure of the accident potential that arises when two dangers—environmental and human—combine. *Risk management* refers to the collective actions that an outdoor leader or organization might take before, during, and after an outing in order to reduce the potential for an accident and in order to minimize the potential for injury or loss. Risk management actions can be grouped into three categories according to whether they occur before, during, or after an incident in the field. The categories are sometimes labeled primary, secondary, and tertiary.

Primary safety procedures are steps an organization can take before an outing begins in order to avoid an accident (or minimize the consequences of one). These preventative or proactive actions may include equipment inspection, pre-trip safety briefings, the training of staff, and a review of potential dangers that might be encountered in the field. Secondary procedures refer to all actions taken during an outing that help minimize the chance of an accident or that constitute a planned response in case of injury. The responsive or reactive measures include first aid, search and rescue, evacuation, and on-site recording of injury data. Tertiary acts refer to everything that is done after an outing in response to an accident or injury. These follow-up or post-hoc practices can include informing next of kin, making contact with legal counsel, and scheduling visits with an injured participant.

As discussed in Chapter One, an accident potential is created when two types of dangers—human and environmental—are present and overlap. For example, a human danger (an inability to swim) combined with an environmental danger (strong undercurrents) creates the risk of drowning. If only one danger and not the other is present (a weak swimmer without undercurrents, or a powerful swimmer with undercurrents), an accident is less likely to occur. When a number of these factors interact, the accident potential of the whole situation can be increased dramatically.

As was also noted in Chapter One, the mere presence of environmental and human dangers does not guarantee that an accident will occur; it only makes it more likely. The precise probability is determined by the number and relative strengths of the dangers that are present. Outdoor leaders cannot possibly predict these percentages with absolute certainty; however, their judgment based on experience can aid in making subjective determinations of the risks. A subjective determination is made by counting the number of dangers, categorizing them as either environmental or human, weighting their strengths, and then doing the math. Although an instructor might not actually calculate a precise probability in the field, it is useful to note how this works. By understanding how the factors relate to one other and contribute to the accident potential, leaders can learn to make better decisions.

When a leader is calculating the risk of hypothermia, for instance, she can note the presence of three environmental dangers (wind, snow, and dropping temperature) and five human dangers (fatigue, hunger, sweaty underclothing, lack of shell clothing, and group inexperience). Because the wind and snow are currently minor factors, the leader assigns them a subjective value of one each. She gives rapidly falling temperature (which is now below zero) a rating of three. She considers fatigue and hunger to be equally weighted as twos. Some students have sweaty clothes, which she considers a two, and because some students lack protective shells, she marks the danger a three. Finally, she gives the group a rating of one for their experience level.

The values are then summed for the environmental (1 + 1 + 3 = 5) and human (2 + 2 + 2 + 3 + 1 = 10) factors. The totals are multiplied by one another (5 X 10 = 50). And the final product tells the leader that the likelihood of hypothermia is subjectively 50 times higher under present conditions than if snow and hunger were the only dangers present (1 X 1 = 1).

While this is not a completely accurate way of predicting probabilities, it does serve as a way to monitor dangers. Perhaps just as importantly, it demonstrates two powerful points: dangers add up, and the interaction between them causes the accident potential to multiply dramatically. The effective leader is well aware of this relationship and can use these rough calculations as part of a fully integrated system of thinking about risk.

Dangers add up, and the interaction between them causes the accident potential to multiply dramatically.

Before assigning values to each danger, a leader must first learn how to weight the various danger strengths. One way to do this is to classify environmental factors as either perils or hazards. *Perils* are the sources of injury or the cause of a loss (rock fall) and can usually be avoided. *Hazards*, on the other hand, are the conditions that accentuate or influence the chance of an injury or loss occurring (traveling near a rock cliff). The risk is created from the interaction of the two dangers; traveling near the rock cliff (a hazard) increases the probability of getting hit by the rock fall (a peril). Understanding this interaction makes the subjective weighting of danger strengths easier and more accurate for leaders.

Effective leaders must be able to recognize both perils and hazards and to use this knowledge to avoid certain risks. Crossing active glaciers to summit a peak, for example, has some obvious perils in the form of crevasses and snow bridges (snow that covers the opening of the crevasse). In this case, a route around a troublesome area might be used to skirt the worst of the perils, even if it doesn't eliminate all of them. When perils cannot be avoided, the hazards must be evaluated. On a glacier, for instance, temperature is a hazard that can affect the likelihood of falling through a snow bridge, which is the peril. The temperature varies according to the time of day, sunlight, and other climactic conditions. As the day warms up, the temperature influences the likelihood that snow bridges will weaken.

Experienced climbers often try to avoid weak snow bridges by choosing a specific time to encounter them. Common practice suggests beginning a summit bid in the dark (with headlamps), getting on top near dawn, and being back to camp by noon (all before temperatures rise markedly). In the heat of the afternoon, the mountaineers may then relax, eat lunch, and watch the snow bridges sag around them, knowing that they have successfully avoided some of the dangers inherent in the climb.

In summary, perils will always be present in adventures.

By knowing how and when these perils are affected by hazards, a leader can learn to reduce the cumulative dangers on either side of the accident equation.

Danger Analysis

Since the interaction of human and environmental dangers gives rise to the risk of an accident, and the interaction of perils and hazards affects the strength of those dangers, effective outdoor leaders must remain vigilant in recognizing and analyzing all the variables they encounter along the way. One way to improve a leader's ability to study the variables is by using a 10-step procedure known as a danger analysis (Priest & Baillie, 1987). This approach may reduce the chance that an accident will happen. In the event an accident does occur, this procedure can help minimize the consequences to acceptable and recoverable levels.

The 10-step process is identified in Figure 2.2 (Priest & Gass, 1998, pp. 90-91), and the following pages provide further explanation of the danger-analysis procedure.

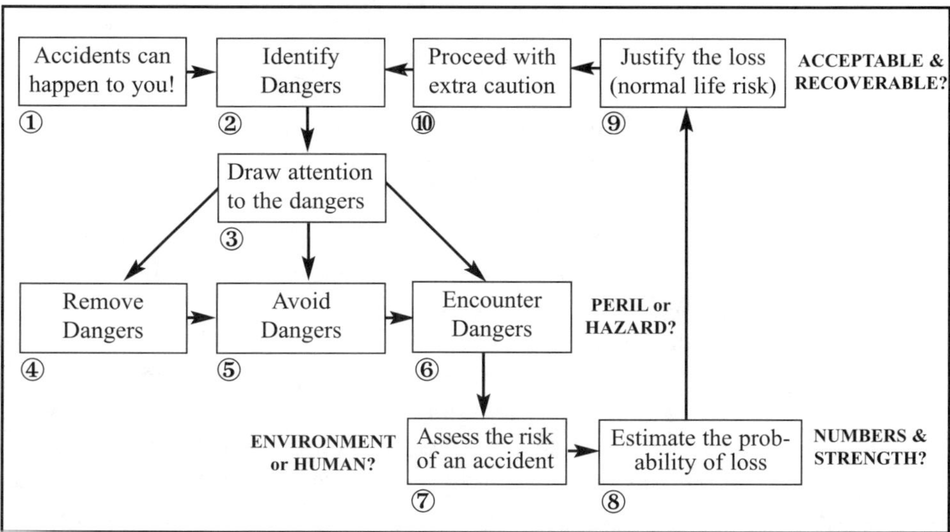

Figure 2.2 *This diagram outlines a 10-step process for analyzing dangers in the outdoors and improving an outdoor leader's decision-making ability. (Adapted from Priest and Baillie, 1987.)*

Admit it can happen to you.

Step 1 Admit it can happen to you. Outdoor leaders with the attitude that an accident can't happen to them are fooling no one but themselves. Despite your best efforts, at some time in your career as an outdoor leader, an accident will occur. The matter is not if, but more importantly, when it will occur and how serious it will be. The key to being ready to deal with a crisis is to first acknowledge your vulnerability.

Step 2 Maintain a continuous search to identify dangers and recognize risks. Outdoor leaders should remain vigilant when looking for dangers in any situation and should imagine what might happen at any time. This is often accomplished by keeping a watchful eye on all suspect circumstances and by continually asking the "what if" question. When many dangers are present, outdoor leaders should be extra alert or cautious and take appropriate actions accordingly.

Step 3 It is not enough for a leader to simply recognize dangers; she must make her students aware of them as well. For example, making students aware of a loose rock (environmental danger) as well as the level of group horseplay that is occurring near the rock (human danger) can potentially prevent an accident (being hit by the rock) from happening. Ultimately, recognition of the potential for an accident is often enough to temporarily alter human behaviors or avoid the environmental dangers so that an accident does not occur.

Step 4 If drawing attention to a danger doesn't work, it might be best to remove the danger entirely (assuming removal does not increase the risk). For instance, removing the loose rock (environmental danger) in the above example makes good sense, provided the rock is not thrown carelessly away to hit someone, or provided its removal does not dislodge an avalanche of many loose rocks. An example of a human danger that might be removed is the student who is seen as being a potential risk to himself or to the other members in the group. In this case, the instructor may ask the individual to leave the outing, provided his removal does not place the group or person in any further danger.

Step 5 If a danger cannot be removed, then the next step is to decide whether or not it can be avoided. This may be as simple as changing a group's travel route so that participants avoid the loose rock. For dangers that are less easily avoided, such as a hazardous river crossing, a leader might decide to change an activity altogether by halting the group completely or even canceling the outing if an encounter looks too dangerous.

Step 6 There will be times when a danger cannot be removed or avoided and simply must be encountered. There are other times when purposely encountering dangers is even desirable. Some dangers, in fact, are considered beneficial; adventurers seek them out. The feeling of overcoming the challenges (and dangers) can be very rewarding and may be one of the main reasons for engaging in the activity.

Even human dangers, such as horseplay, can be good under some conditions. Consider a playful water fight: It may help cool people on a hot day and also improve moods and relationships within the group. In other words, some potential dangers can be positive, provided they are properly encountered (alone and not in combination with other dangers).

Effective leaders encounter dangers in a well-reasoned and appropriate manner. If they are diligent about safety, they will stay continually alert to the hazards that can make the unavoidable perils even more dangerous. By choosing to encounter the perils at times when hazards are at a minimum, they reduce the risk of an accident.

Step 7 Once it is clear that a group will be encountering a danger, the leader must assess the risks associated with that danger. By identifying dangers as either environmental (based on the surroundings) or human (based on the group), the leader determines the potential for overlap, as seen in the accident-potential equation. Where dangers combine and overlap exists, the risk of an accident increases. The effective outdoor leader recognizes this fact and is always on the alert for conditions where such an overlap or interaction exists.

Step 8 If overlap seems imminent, the leader must estimate the probability of an accident before proceeding. In order to do this, the leader should address two questions. How much overlap can be expected? And how probable is it that the combination will lead to some kind of loss? Recall that more numerous and stronger dangers lead to a greater likelihood that an accident will occur. In order to determine the probability of loss, the leader should note the number of dangers in the human and environmental categories. Absolute numbers do not necessarily mean that accidents are proportionately likely, but when more dangers are present, more combinations are possible, and consequently, the probability of an accident is greater.

To illustrate, let's go back to the introductory story. The glacier-travel group was going to have to encounter certain dangers no matter what choice they made. However, there were more dangers present that evening than there would be in the morning. Human dangers included fatigued, hungry, and inexperienced students. Environmental dangers included a crevassed glacier, multiple snow bridges (softened by sunlight throughout the day), and uneven terrain. If the group proceeded on to the hut that evening, several environmental and human dangers would be combined. Even without the math, an effective leader can recognize that the accident potential in this situation is fairly high.

On the other hand, if the group chose to camp for the night and proceed the next morning, the probability changes. The participants would be rested and well fed. Further, the snow bridges would be stronger, having cooled and solidified during the night. As a result, though environmental and human dangers still exist, their numbers and strengths have been reduced. The likelihood of an accident is therefore lessened.

Step 9 If the risk of an accident appears probable (though still, of course, not an absolute certainty) and a leader decides to encounter the dangers anyway, he must be able to justify that the outcome of such an accident is both acceptable and recoverable. One way to do this is to compare the expected outcome with organization's mission statement. If the mission of the program is to provide safe, educational experiences, for example, it might be difficult to justify any serious accident. On the other hand, if an organization's mission is to develop leadership skills through adventure activities, a higher level of risk (and higher probability of an accident) might be acceptable. This concept is discussed in greater detail in chapters three and six.

Another way to evaluate whether or not a potential accident is acceptable is by comparing the risk posed by the dangers with the amount of risk that is present in everyday living. Normal life risk refers to the chance of injury people are exposed to in daily existence. A 20-year safety study from Project Adventure (Furlong, Jillings, LaRhette & Ryan, 1995, p. 5) reported a rate of 4.33 injuries per million hours of exposure. The study commented that "roughly speaking, participating in a Project Adventure program is approximately as risky as working in the fields of real estate, insurance, or finance," which have rates of 4.5 injuries per million hours. By comparing accident data from outdoor adventure-based programs with data from everyday normal life activities, outdoor leaders can sometimes justify risks in relation to reality.

In another study, Higgins (1981) found that there was a lower ratio of disabling injuries associated with Outward Bound courses than there was from either driving an automobile or playing college football. Meyer (1979) also reported fewer deaths due to outdoor adventures than due to automobile accidents. From these data comparisons (which were adjusted for amount of time involved and number of people exposed to the dangers), adventure experiences again appear less risky than some of the behaviors associated with everyday living.

Admittedly, these comparisons are limited to only major injuries that occurred in a few well-known programs. In order to make broader comparisons, further research is needed that covers minor injuries as well and that includes a wider variety of adventure programs. Such data collection has been conducted since the early 1980s by Alan Hale's (Inter) National Safety Network (ISN) and has recently been taken over by the Association for Experiential Education (AEE). Initial reports from ISN and AEE continue to suggest that participants in many adventure programs are exposed to lower levels of risk than they normally experience in everyday living.

Step 10 If the outdoor leader decides that the probability of an accident is low or that the loss from an accident will be acceptable and recoverable, he may choose to proceed. But he should do so with extra caution, always prepared for the worst-case scenario. Around the next bend may be new dangers and more opportunities to recognize, assess, weigh, and evaluate. A good leader stays alert, continually searching for new dangers, noticing how they combine with existing dangers, and continually assessing how they change the levels of risk.

Factors that Affect the Danger Analysis

Now that the danger-analysis process has been described, it is worthwhile to note that certain factors can inhibit the successful use of this procedure. As shown in Figure 2.3,

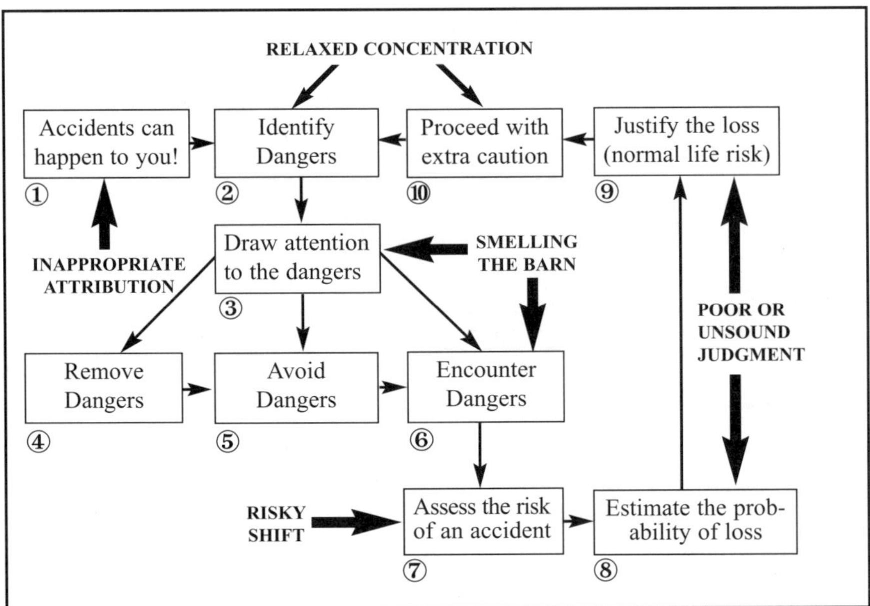

Figure 2.3 *The author identifies five barriers or inhibiting factors that affect the danger-analysis procedure.*

these factors include inappropriate attribution, relaxed concentration, smelling the barn, risky shift, and poor or unsound judgment (Priest & Gass, 1998, pp. 92-93). Although these factors affect the process in different ways, the overall result (i.e., higher probability of an accident) can be the same.

Inappropriate attribution refers to the tendency people have to take credit for (or internally attribute) good happenings and to place the blame (externally attribute) on something other than themselves (such as bad weather or faulty equipment) when things go wrong. This behavior can prevent outdoor leaders from taking the first step in the danger-analysis procedure: They may simply refuse to admit that an accident could happen to them.

Relaxed concentration involves dropping one's guard due to fatigue, pride, or carelessness. Once an outdoor leader drops her guard, she is less likely to be constantly looking for dangers and will not be sufficiently alert to proceed with caution. This behavior is often seen in parties descending from mountain peaks, and is also commonly seen in groups egressing from a river run (sprained ankles are more common once the paddling is over than they are at the access or "carry in" when people are more alert).

Familiarity with dangers can also breed contempt, as outdoor leaders can become desensitized to ongoing dangers. For instance, spending all day skiing in potential avalanche conditions without evidence of any slides may incorrectly and positively reinforce the belief that the slopes are not really that dangerous. This phenomenon is also seen when an instructor teaches a course in a specific area again and again. The newness is gone, the route is less stimulating, his concentration is relaxed, and consequently, he may be less vigilant in assessing the dangers around him.

"Smelling the barn" is a behavior shared by horses, cows, and some outdoor leaders. It is the act of rushing to get to a known site or the end of a trip. This can occur when a group is attempting to maintain a schedule, or it can happen when participants see that the end is in sight. As a result, outdoor leaders may forget to point out dangers, or they may tend to encounter dangers that they might normally remove or avoid. Given the peer pressure to get home to a warm shower or a

hot meal, these goals can ultimately become more persuasive than safety.

Risky shift is based on research showing that groups tend to make riskier decisions than individuals do (Meier, 1981). There are several ways this common phenomenon can happen. Novice group members may be reluctant to express their fears. Courage is, after all, a socially desirable trait, and if others don't seem afraid, a group member may become willing to accept higher risks than she would on her own. Also, in risk-taking situations experienced members tend to be more bold and outspoken than conservative novices, and therefore may have a greater influence on the decision-making process. Additionally, some people may abandon their responsibility to engage in the decision-making process, transferring that responsibility instead to the leader (often without the leader's knowledge). Without understanding these factors, an instructor might unwittingly lead a group into dangers beyond their abilities: No one wishes to appear cowardly, yet many are reluctant to admit being in over their heads. As a result, risky shift leads the group and the leaders to underestimate risk.

Poor or unsound judgment inhibits many aspects of outdoor leadership, and the effect it has on safety is no exception. Faulty judgment will inhibit a leader's ability to estimate the probability of loss. It can also affect a leader's ability to justify that loss. Since good judgment is so important to safe adventure programming, outdoor leaders must evaluate their own judgments on a continual basis. A good leader should also consider seeking the open and honest critique of colleagues. Although this process may feel threatening, judgment can be greatly improved if leaders are willing to learn from each other. Ideally, leaders ought to be able to truthfully discuss their close calls, near misses, epic journeys, and embarrassing mistakes without fear of retribution from their peers or administrators.

The Importance of Judgment

When important information is missing, vague, or unknown, the ability to problem-solve or make good decisions gets increasingly difficult. The course of action may even stall temporarily until new information becomes available.

Judgment is the process of drawing on past experiences in order to provide the necessary information to move forward again. With new information (obtained from judgment, based on experience), the problem-solving or decision-making processes can continue (Priest, 1988).

Because uncertainty is the basic ingredient of all adventures, judgment is a critical attribute of outdoor leaders. Good judgment is an indispensable tool for estimating uncertainty, substituting for missing information, guessing about the vague, and predicting in place of the unknown. Effective outdoor leaders use their judgment to solve problems and make decisions under conditions of uncertainty (Petzoldt, 1984, p. 42).

Good judgment is an indispensable tool for estimating uncertainty, substituting for missing information, guessing about the vague, and predicting in place of the unknown.

But why is it that some people do not seem to learn from their own or others' mistakes? Why is it that some experienced outdoor enthusiasts make obviously poor choices? Judgment is not the same as experience. Instead, it is a cycle of three processes: inductive, deductive, and evaluative reflection. It is through these three steps that leaders improve their judgment and enhance their decision-making abilities.

The first step, *inductive reflection*, is used to create general concepts from specific experiences. For example, over the course of their lifetimes, outdoor leaders may walk or ski on various types of snow under all kinds of conditions. From this collection of experience, they will induce some general rules about snow: it melts when the temperature is warm and refreezes when the temperature drops. As a leader gains more experience, he may also learn that when temperatures are extremely cold and dry, the snow is so unconsolidated that he will sink to the ground if he attempts to cross a field. On the other hand, if he wishes to cross the same field on an early spring morning, the snow is often so firm that it will hold his weight and he'll have no problem walking across the surface. The more experiences people gain, the more accurate their general concepts become.

This increased accuracy comes about from the correct utilization of both deductive and evaluative reflections. *Deductive reflection* is used to make specific predictions based on general concepts. Continuing with the snow example, an outdoor leader may be asked to predict what snow conditions will be like on the other (north) side of a ridge he will soon be traversing. If he notes only that the temperature is above freezing (with the sun shining brightly), he may predict that the snow will be slushy. However, when his group arrives on the other side (where the sun and wind have created a very different effect), the snow might be extremely hard packed. In this case his prediction (deduction), which was based on a general concept, proved incorrect (and the group would have been very lucky to have brought their crampons).

Evaluative reflection is used to analyze the accuracy of the deductive prediction (such as the consistency of the north-slope snow pack). A leader can use this analysis as a new experience for further induction, which will ultimately improve his knowledge of general concepts. In this example, the outdoor leader should evaluate why his prediction was off. Once it becomes clear that the new snow conditions happen to be on a highly windy, non-sunny side of the ridge, he can refine his rules: even if temperatures are warm, snow can be extremely hard-packed if it receives little sun and if very cold winds are continuously blowing over its surface.

The trick to evaluative reflection is not just in accurately reinforcing correct predictions, but also in one's ability to analyze incorrect ones. Consider the positive reinforcement of repeatedly walking out onto high-risk, unstable snow slopes and not experiencing an avalanche. If one does not evaluate why she "got away with it" each time, she may become complacent about all snow slopes and wrongly assume the risk of avalanche is low or non-existent. Inevitably this will result in an accident or cost someone a life.

The judgment cycle diagrammed in Figure 2.4 explains how these three reflective activities (inductive, deductive and evaluative) fit together (Priest, 1990).

We can examine the stages of the judgment cycle by using the common activity of backcountry navigation (Priest & Gass, 1998, P. 257). Consider all the information and experiences one receives when first learning to navigate: map reading, compass use, and off-trail orienteering. As these specific experiences accumulate they become available for inductive reflection. The resulting general concepts are then stored in memory where they can be retrieved for future use, (e.g., in interpreting contour lines, when adjusting for mag-

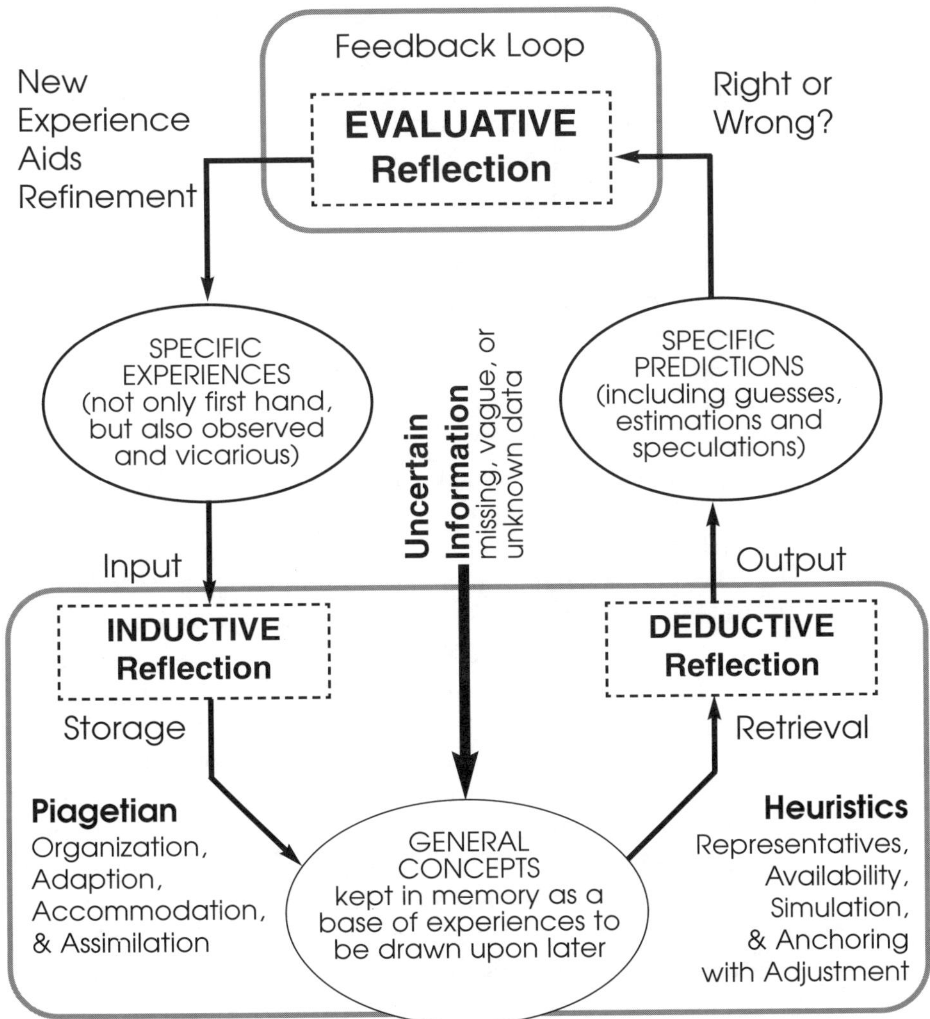

Figure 2.4 *The cycle of experience-based judgment shows how reflection can be used to improve a leader's ability to predict or "fill in the blanks."*

netic declination, or purposefully "aiming-off").

When an outdoor leader is faced with the task of navigating from a ridge-top down to a camp by the river, she can retrieve the general concepts from memory and output them in order to deductively reflect and create a specific course of action. She might, for instance, decide to walk along the ridge to a low saddle (following the contour lines from the map), drop down into the woods (on an adjusted magnetic bearing), head for a point deliberately upstream of the camp (by aiming -off), and then follow the river downstream to her final destination. After arriving at camp, the leader can evaluate the relative success of the exercise and reflect on how things may have been done differently.

Suppose this leader had not reached the river at the correct place and had instead intersected the river downstream of camp. Analysis of this process can help her determine the source of the error. By reflecting on the outcome of this experience, the leader creates new information that will ultimately enhance the general concepts held in memory. As a result, her navigation skills will be improved the next time around.

In summary, inductive reflection creates a "base" of experiences for outdoor leaders. The base is held in long-term memory as a complex map of general concepts. The map contains facts (confirmed through repeated judgment cycles), beliefs (partially supported by experience), and hypotheses (as yet untested), all of which are arranged in relation to one another by many common connections (same topic, similar outcomes, and so on). When uncertainty is present (information is missing, vague, or unknown) an outdoor leader can access the memory map of general concepts and retrieve those facts, beliefs, and hypotheses that are deemed most relevant to the circumstances. The information is then subjected to deductive reflection, and specific predictions are created to fill in for the uncertainties. Once again, evaluating the effectiveness of these predictions and analyzing their accuracy help to hone the outdoor leader's experiences through the ongoing judgment cycle.

Learning to Improve Judgment

Gathering experience is obviously a critical activity for effective outdoor leaders. Instructors benefit when they have a breadth and depth of intensive and extensive experiences from as many sources as possible, including both first-hand experiences as well as those obtained from others. However, experience alone does not guarantee that outdoor leaders will have sound judgment.

Experience without reflection rarely results in learning;

hence the importance of induction, deduction, and evaluation is obvious. It is worth examining these three processes a little deeper, therefore, to learn how they influence the judgment cycle.

Inductive reflection is guided by the organization, adaptation, assimilation, and accommodation theories of Piaget, who studied the cognitive development of children. Deductive reflection is guided by the rules of thumb or heuristics of representativeness, availability, simulation, and anchoring (with adjustment). Evaluative reflection is the key to honing one's judgment and is also the secret to developing judgment in others. Let's consider each of these three processes in more detail.

The Induction Process

The inductive activities of input, inductive reflection, and storage are guided by organization, adaptation, assimilation, and accommodation. *Organization* suggests that information is handled sequentially. This influences the way information is mapped into memory and affects the way these maps relate to other memory maps. *Adaptation* refers to the way organized memory maps change in accordance with changing situations. Adaptation is said to be the root of learning. *Assimilation* is one method of adaptation, as new and similar information is fit to an existing memory map. *Accommodation* is another way of adapting when an existing memory map is modified to incorporate new but different information.

For example, from repeated experiences an outdoor leader may have induced simple concepts like "side-stepping on a slope prevents slipping." However, the same person can learn that digging your boot heels into the slope provides similar results. This new and similar information is "assimilated" into the existing map as a way to preventing slipping. As a result, new information is input and stored into memory.

The Deduction Process

The deductive activities of retrieval, deductive reflection, and output are guided by representativeness, availability, simulation, and anchoring (Kahneman, Slovic, & Tversky, 1982).

Representativeness is the extent to which information from a past situation represents or matches information needed for the current situation. *Availability* is the ease with which specific information can be brought to mind. *Simulation* refers to the related ability of imagining or constructing scenarios from retrieved information. *Anchoring* (with adjustment) is the weighting of the information's importance at the time it was obtained. Anchoring also refers to the interpretation of new information in light of early or already obtained information.

Outdoor leaders tend to search their memories for "representative" instances that are as similar as possible to their present situations. Consider, for example, a leader who is on a whitewater paddling trip during a high run-off period. Each piece of information retrieved from the leader's memory map is compared with and assessed for how well it represents the actual river being run. Past trips on rivers of similar difficulty, or on rivers that were run during high run off, are likely to be the memory maps most heavily used for deductive reflection. They are most representative of what the leader can expect in the current situation.

Leaders are also most likely to be swayed by information that is most recently "available" to them and are less likely to be influenced by information that was obtained a long time ago. The same is true if the information had little versus considerable bearing on their lives. For example, a person's perception of the risk posed by lightning is likely to be influenced by media reports of recent fatalities due to lightning. A traumatic personal experience or recent negative information may also lead to an over-sensitivity and higher perception of risk. On the other hand, recent positive information can lead to an underestimation of the danger posed by lightning strikes.

Kahneman, Slovic, and Tversky (1982, p.13) explain the "simulation" heuristic as it applies to the risks of an expedition "by imagining contingencies with which the expedition is not equipped to cope. If many such difficulties are vividly portrayed, the expedition can be made to appear exceedingly dangerous, although the ease with which disasters are imagined need not reflect their actual likelihood. Conversely, the risk involved in an undertaking may be grossly underestimated if some possible dangers are either difficult to conceive of, or simply do not come to mind."

First impressions are an excellent example of how anchoring (with adjustments) works. For instance, outdoor leaders are likely to put a lot of faith in their first observation of an individual and then temper their opinions from that position by using further observations. If the individual initially appears confident, it is likely that the outdoor leader will continue to see the person in that light, regardless of subsequent deviations (unless the departure is blatant). This anchoring is desirable, because a reference point is available from which to judge and refine judgments. The jeopardy, of course, lies in the first impression being false. In the event future information sheds new and significantly different light on the situation, a modified or adjusted impression will result.

Sound judgment cannot be taught, but it can be developed and improved.

The Evaluative Process

Lastly, the evaluative process is the secret to successfully enhancing judgment. Sound judgment cannot be taught, but it can be developed and improved, provided evaluative reflection is conducted. This assumption is typically based on the premise that one learns best from mistakes. This publication, in fact, provides ample lessons from leaders who have learned from their own mistakes or the misjudgments of others.

Unfortunately the premise is somewhat flawed. There is just as much to be learned from achievement as failure, from analyzing why things didn't go wrong or why they went so well. Figuring out "what went wrong" often seems to be easier than determining "what was right." For this reason, outdoor leaders commonly avoid evaluating successful endeavors and choose instead to analyze only their errors. Unfortunately, if they fail to analyze their achievements, they miss a golden opportunity for learning.

The following suggestions can be used to help outdoor leaders hone their judgment:

- Learn about and reflect on a program's rules as well as the exceptions to those rules.
- Gather as much information as possible from lectures, historical case studies, and horror stories of other leaders.

- Observe other leaders and how they use judgment.
- Develop a questioning attitude and inquire about the predictions other leaders make.
- Recall personal near misses and share them openly with others.
- Consider and reflect on the analyses of personal mistakes given by others.
- React (verbally or by written word) to dilemmas that were posed by other leaders.
- Keep a logbook (of experiences) and a judgment journal (reflecting on those experiences).
- Get as much experience as possible and take advantage of every opportunity that comes your way. Never turn down any reasonable chance to lead.
- Take a group of peers on an expedition and get their honest feedback regarding your performance.
- Undertake practical internships with several programs and ask for someone to observe and give advice.
- Become an apprentice to an expert leader. Ask the mentor to pass on responsibility in a gradual manner. Seek advice and feedback regarding your performance.
- Above all, evaluate and thoroughly reflect on every experience you have, the positive as well as the negative.

Summary

Leadership is a blend of many different skills. Hard skills (technical, safety, environmental) are more tangible and easier to learn; soft skills (organizational, instructional, facilitational) are less obvious and fairly difficult to develop; and meta skills (flexible leadership style, problem-solving and decision-making ability, judgment based on experience, effective communication, and ethical behaviors) are the glue that binds the hard and soft skills together to create a more effective leader. Safety and judgment turn up repeatedly as the most important of these skill areas.

Safety (or the ability to assess and minimize risk) involves the assortment of procedures an organization or outdoor leader can use to protect clients and prevent accidents that might cause injury or loss. Most accidents occur when human and environmental dangers combine and interact at the same moment to create an accident potential. Although the accident potential can identify the likelihood of an accident happening, it does not provide a certainty that one will occur. Nonetheless, the more dangers present, the greater the risk.

Dangers can be classified as perils or hazards. Perils are the sources of loss, and hazards are the conditions that accentuate the chance of a loss. If perils must be encountered, they are best met when hazards are low and therefore the least influential.

Judgment is an experience-based application of the brain's ability to reason by a cycle of three reflections. Inductive reflection is a collection of specific experiences (first hand, observed, and vicarious) that creates a map of general concepts. These concepts are stored in memory (as an experience) and can be drawn upon later. When information that is needed for problem-solving or decision-making is uncertain, missing, vague, or unknown, the memory maps are used. Relevant general concepts are searched for, and when found, they are subjected to deductive reflection. This, in turn, provides information that can be used to fill in the blanks. The final output is the estimation, substitution, guess, or prediction that is later is evaluated and reflected upon in order to determine its accuracy. Ultimately, a new experience is created and used for further cycled reflection and overall improvement of judgment.

Using the information provided in this chapter, we can return to the opening scenario and consider the decision that had to be made on the glacier. The leaders were able to recognize the dangers around them. They assessed the risks, evaluated their options, and considered the accident potential for each choice. Because the instructors had experience with similar groups in similar situations, they were able to retrieve useful information from their memory maps. By using their combined judgment, they were able to make a reasonable prediction that continuing on would not be wise. In the end, the group organized as much equipment as it could prior to going to bed, and early the next morning they began their hike to the hut: well-fed, well-rested and on the surface of the frozen snow (and solid snow bridges). After reaching the hut, the leaders reflected on their decision and added the new successful experience to their continually growing bank of general concepts.

Hindsight is 20:20. In their report on the University of Alaska Anchorage's Ptarmigan Peak accident, and over concern for possible public and media responses to their findings, Williamson, Ratz and Miller (1997, p.1) wrote:

> *Mistakes and accidents in mountaineering, as in all endeavors, cannot be eliminated. When reviewing the mistakes ... it is essential to consider the intentions of those who made them, and how, in the long run, the systems can be improved so that the future management of the inherent risks will be viewed as acceptable.*

Outdoor leaders must remember that even the best judgment and the safest leadership will not prevent all injuries; there are simply too many uncontrollable dangers in the outdoors. Removing the entire spectrum of risks, however, would negate the learning potential of adventure experiences. In fact, without uncertainty and risk there would be no adventure.

With effective outdoor leadership, unreasonable risks can be minimized and learning opportunities optimized. By learning from your own as well as others' successes and mistakes, you can improve your judgment and enhance your leadership abilities. That, in essence, is the prudent choice for all adventure programs.

Learning from Ptarmigan Peak

Rewriting an Organizational Risk Management Plan

by Deborah Ajango

In the summer of 1997, two students in a University of Alaska Anchorage (UAA) mountaineering course died from a catastrophic fall during a university field outing. Over the next 12 months, the outdoor education department conducted an extensive examination of the program's risk management plan to find out how such a tragedy could have occurred and what might be done to prevent future accidents. This chapter identifies six components of an effective risk management plan and uses UAA's experience as a case study for reflection on the importance of making conscious choices in the management of risk.

It is not realistic to think that we can ever prevent all accidents in outdoor education. Nevertheless, as outdoor educators we have a responsibility to our students to reduce the potential for accidents as much as possible and to lessen the consequences associated with each. Most of us probably think we are already doing this. We hire good people, follow accepted practices, and warn our students of the dangers inherent in outdoor activities. But are we really doing enough? This was the question the University of Alaska Anchorage's (UAA's) outdoor education department faced in the aftermath of a tragic accident. Our program was in place, our risk management plan had been implemented and reviewed, we had received acclaim for our fine work. And a catastrophic accident happened anyway.

UAA's outdoor education program began in 1972 as Alaska Wilderness Studies. In its early years it operated more like a climbing club than a formal academic program, but gradually it grew and matured until, by the 1990s, more than 1000 students per year enrolled in its classes. The department's accident rate (which is measured in number of incidents per participant numbers x course hours) was comparable to other outdoor programs. Although there had been a variety of minor injuries over the years—scrapes, tweaked knees, and even broken bones—no incidents had been serious enough in nearly 10 years to require in-patient hospitalization.

The program was committed to quality and continually strove to become ever more professional. In June 1997 it received national accreditation from the Association for Experiential Education. With this national recognition, department staff had good reason to believe that the program was moving in the right direction and all was well. One month later, on the north couloir of Ptarmigan Peak, we learned differently.

The accident on Ptarmigan Peak claimed two lives; 12 other participants, including the two instructors, were injured. The magnitude of the tragedy was far reaching and the widespread waves of pain immense. The community, the university, and the department were stunned. Although UAA had a crisis-response plan in place, no one was fully prepared for such an event. After the initial confusion and numbness began to subside, the program and university, still shocked that something like this could have happened, went looking for answers.

Over the next 12 months, we critically evaluated every aspect of our outdoor education program. We wanted to know which, if any, of our practices might have contributed to the fall. Also, as we identified changes that would help prevent another mountaineering accident, we wondered if there might be similar changes that could improve our non-mountaineering courses as well. Were there other areas of the program that, although not cause for immediate concern, could potentially contribute to problems in the future?

We listened to advice from far and wide, much of it contradictory. In general, there seemed to be two basic schools of thought. Many people blamed the instructors and said that we should reevaluate our hiring and training policies. Hire the right people and you won't have accidents, they maintained. Others blamed management and recommended that we impose more policies and procedures as a way of controlling what happens in the field. Both of these points of view had merit, but neither, we felt, held all the answers.

Instructor judgment is obviously a critical part of what happens in the field. A well-trained, experienced leader can greatly minimize the potential of an accident. But there is a danger in relying on instructor judgment as the sole source of an organization's risk management strategy. Safety in the outdoors requires back-up plans. To prevent a climbing anchor from failing, for instance, redundancy is used to provide a safety net, thus mitigating the potential for disaster. We believed the same should be true for an instructor; a safety net should exist in case an instructor makes a mistake. Although we hope and expect to always "hire the best" employees, it is unrealistic to think that every hire will be ideal and every instructor will perform without error. Because instructors and managers are human, we cannot expect perfection. Sooner or later something will go wrong.

A safety net should exist in case an instructor makes a mistake.

To compensate for the potential of human error, organizations and administrators are sometimes tempted to impose multiple policies. They hope that by restricting the choices an instructor or manager has to make, the likelihood of misjudgment will be minimized. But anyone who has worked in the field of outdoor education understands that, because of the continually changing environments, personalities, and conditions, no rule can apply to every situation.

Consequently, when we assessed our risk management and accident prevention strategies, we did so believing it was important to consider and enhance both of these aspects (instructor judgment as well as policies) but to rely totally on neither. We still wanted to encourage and reward individual excellence, but we also wanted to create a system that provided backup in the event of unintended human error. We chose an approach that would provide checks and balances, minimize the chance of an accident, and eliminate the potential of catastrophic failure.

Our process involved dozens of people and almost as many points of view. We created a *Plan of Action*, circulated it to more than a hundred outdoor professionals from around the nation, and asked for feedback. Locally, we held meetings to evaluate nearly every aspect of the program, including our hiring and field practices, student preparation methods, communication and evaluation systems, and venue selection process.

By the end of the year, our overhaul was complete. We had changed our name from Alaska Wilderness Studies to Alaska Outdoor and Experiential Education (AOEE), a name that more accurately reflects our mission. We updated our instructor hiring process, modified our instructor orientation and training procedures, changed our pre-course education and preparation steps, revamped our venue lists, produced checklists to minimize the chance that items or procedures might be overlooked or forgotten, revised our field policies and procedures, and created backups for many of the practices that were already in place. Recognizing that a one-time revamp was not an end in itself, we also built in steps to ensure that the program and its risk management system would be reviewed and assessed on an ongoing basis.

Looking back, we recognize that we have learned a lot as a result of the accident on Ptarmigan Peak. In grappling with these issues we learned what makes an effective risk management strategy, what decisions need to be made to implement it, and how important it is to continually monitor an organization's goals and practices to maintain synergy between them.

This chapter identifies some of the main lessons learned from the accident and subsequent review process. It is my hope that this information will prove useful to any reader who wants to more closely examine the primary and secondary factors that can affect the quality and success of an organizational risk management plan.

Components of a Management System

A risk management system should address six key features of an organization's identity: *why, what, who, where, when* and *how*. Together, these components can be used to create a system that enhances a student's experience, decreases the likelihood of an accident, and ultimately reduces an agency's exposure to legal liability. Although most risk management plans include at least some of these components, many either lack or are lax in one or more. An effective system, on the other hand, pays careful attention to all of them.

- **Why** — program philosophy, mission statement, and risk management goals
- **What** — selection of course activities and curriculum
- **Who** — selection and training of staff and participants
- **Where** — venue selection
- **When** — course scheduling and resource considerations
- **How** — accepted field practices

Ideally, as each feature is discussed, decided upon, and formalized, it should be documented and organized into a policy and procedure manual. But even if an organization chooses not to craft a formal document, it is important that none of the components is forgotten or overlooked.

WHY: Philosophy, Mission, and Goals

Outdoor professionals and organizations have many things in common, but differences exist nonetheless. A mission statement, for example, summarizes an organization's reason for being, and those reasons can vary widely. One agency's mission might be to promote personal growth in teenagers, another's to improve technical skills in adults, and a third might focus on providing environmental education to students. The common factor in all mission statements is that they provide guidance for the organization's operations, guidance that should extend to the organization's risk management plan as well.

It is not uncommon for organizations in the same profession to have different missions. Borrowing an analogy from Jasper Hunt (Chapter Six), it is clear that though a commercial pilot and a military pilot have similar professions, they have very different missions. Accordingly, they face a different level of risk each day, and that difference is acceptable because of the different duties they are expected to perform.

The same may be true of outdoor leaders who work for two different organizations. Though both might deal with similar professional hazards,[1] their field practices (and the amount of risk that is considered acceptable) may differ greatly, depending on the courses they teach, on the clientele they serve, and ultimately, on each agency's mission.

Accordingly, it is worthwhile for an organization to clarify and identify its own mission along with its philosophy regarding risk and risk management. What place does safety have in the organization's mission? How does adventure and challenge fit in? How safe are field staff expected to be? When do the risks outweigh the benefits? By answering these questions and clarifying a program's philosophy, an organization makes a clear statement about its approach to risk and what it expects from its employees.

The promise of an "adventure of a lifetime" may suggest that a higher level of risk is acceptable as long as the risk enhances the adventure.

Ambiguity is more common than we realize. Take, for example, a program that advertises in its brochure that it will provide clients with "the adventure of a lifetime." What exactly does this mean? The organization may think it is promoting safety first, but in many ways it may actually present safety as a secondary goal: in its literature, in its curriculum, and consequently, to its employees and students.

The promise of an "adventure of a lifetime" may suggest, in fact, that a higher level of risk is acceptable as long as the risk enhances the adventure. An instructor who works for the organization, in turn, may decide to change venues and take a high-functioning group of students to a more difficult location in order to challenge them. Or, if the group was quick to learn beginning skills, the instructor may move them rapidly on to intermediate or advanced techniques. The instructor may recognize that the group is being exposed to increased risks; however, she also believes the risks can be managed and ultimately the end (providing an exciting and challenging experience) justifies the means.

Like most outdoor programs, UAA's had always promoted safety. But in retrospect, I believe the message may have been too subtle for potential students and for program staff. In some of the old program literature, for instance, the prominent goal often listed in the course syllabus was "to have

[1] *In Chapter Two, Simon Priest draws a distinction between perils and hazards. Throughout the remainder of this book, however, the two terms are used interchangeably.*

fun," and at times the terms *risk management*, and *student/ instructor safety* or *well-being* were used sparingly, if at all.

Consequently, to declare and solidify the high priority AOEE had assigned to risk management, the department decided to create and formalize a risk management goal and put it in writing. We reasoned that if managers, field instructors, and students could see the goal and were continually reminded of the program's dedication to it, "safety first" would become a true priority and an attitude rather than an assumption.

Safety can never be assumed.

By using existing resources (such as *Administrative Practices of Accredited Adventure Programs*) and examining other agencies' risk management statements, we created a new section for our policy and procedure manual, calling it "AOEE's Approach to Risk Management." The section reads, in part, "At AOEE, our goal is … to successfully administer courses … with no injuries to students or instructors, and to provide students with a high-quality education while maintaining the greatest risk management possible." The section also identifies some of the steps the program uses to help achieve that goal.

We now require all new employees to know and understand the program's risk management goal as well as the department's mission statement, and we discuss these sections of the manual at length during new-employee orientations. This change has helped to establish and communicate the fact that the program's mission is central to all it does. AOEE is serious about its approach to risk management; safety can never be assumed.

WHAT: Activities and Curricula

All organizations make choices about which activities to offer, from backpacking to rock climbing to mountaineering. A good question to ask at such times is: Is the activity worth the risk? An organization that is concerned with risk management should select an activity because it supports the program's mission and not simply because it is marketable or because some instructors think it sounds fun. Bungee jumping may be a completely appropriate activity for an organization whose primary goal is to provide clients with a thrill or short-term adventure. However, the same activity seems incompatible with an organization whose goal is to provide environmental or outdoor education.

Once potential activities are identified, an organization should consider whether or not it will be able to successfully administer them in a safe manner. Are adequate resources (staff and equipment) available? Can the risks be minimized appropriately while working with a preferred clientele?

To address some of these questions and concerns, and to help field instructors and students succeed, it is a good idea to create a comprehensive curriculum and identify expected outcomes for each course or activity. The benefits of this exercise are threefold. A well-crafted curriculum helps students select the courses most appropriate for their goals, experience, and fitness levels. It assists instructors in structuring their classes around a proven sequence, and provides them with a checklist so they won't forget anything important. And administrators can more effectively evaluate whether or not the identified field activities enhance (rather than conflict with) their program's mission statement, risk management philosophy, and overall client/course objectives.

A well-crafted curriculum identifies key points that can be covered in a given amount of time. It also includes sequencing; as a course progresses, students should be prepared mentally and physically for increasingly difficult tasks. The written guidelines reduce the temptation for instructors to skip ahead and provide more advanced training to students who have minimal experience and have not yet developed and mastered fundamental skills or judgment. Some instructors may complain that course guides feel stifling, but those employees should be encouraged to be creative in their methods of delivery. Ultimately, each instructor can develop his or her own style to achieve success.

The process of reviewing and modifying our curricula turned out to be lively and informative. We sought input from dozens of outdoor enthusiasts and professionals both from within and outside the university. Debates were held to identify the most essential topics that an instructor would be required to cover in each course and that realistically could be taught in the specified time frame. After 28 separate meetings, a core curriculum eventually was identified for every AOEE course. The new course guides provide quality control and reliability. Because an instructor must follow an outline, each participant can confidently know what will be included in a course. Further, the department can rest assured that a student who has successfully completed the basic curriculum covered all of the foundational skills and prerequisites needed for upper-division classes.

The department's Mountaineering I course, for example, was rewritten to include the following subjects:

1) Introduction to risk assessment and hazard evaluation
2) Clothing, safety, and climbing equipment
3) Physiological responses to the mountaineering environment
4) Four-season alpine camping
5) Backcountry navigation
6) Ice axe use
7) Ropes and knots
8) Belay techniques
9) Ascent and descent techniques, and
10) Roped travel

Previous backpacking experience is a requirement for enrolling in the course, so little time is spent teaching basic backpacking skills. Course outcomes are based on proficiency of subject matter, and instructors are not allowed to introduce more advanced skills in the event a group gets through the basic-skills list earlier than anticipated. Students are required to successfully complete this course before they can enroll in Mountaineering II, so the Mountaineering II instructor can feel confident that all students have some competency in the basic skills and are adequately prepared for the intermediate curriculum and terrain.

We believe the new outlines have improved the quality of our services, and AOEE now maintains individual course content guides for each of thc roughly 45 courses we teach. In order to ensure that the guides remain up-to-date with changing technology, the department's Risk Management Advisory Committee reviews them at least every three years.

An example of a course outline and course objectives is included in Appendix A. Although this guide may be more comprehensive than many organizations need, it is included as a sample of a well-thought-out agenda or script.

WHO: Instructors, Volunteers, and Students

The most skilled climber or rafter, or the person who has the most certifications, does not always make the best teacher.

The "who" of an agency includes at least three kinds of people: instructors, volunteers, and students. Each of these categories has a unique relationship to the organization that is worth examining.

Instructors

Field instructors are key to an outdoor agency's ability to minimize the potential for an accident. Even if all aspects of risk management have been considered and properly addressed, the system will be jeopardized if poorly qualified leaders are hired to take groups into the field. But how do you recognize a good instructor? Which qualities are most important? What should an agency look for when selecting and hiring staff?

Outdoor educators know that the most skilled climber or rafter, or the person who has the most certifications, does not always make the best teacher. Certifications are certainly valuable; however, an instructor's judgment and decision-making skills are equally, if not more, important. The best instructors have a healthy mix of the qualities Simon Priest categorizes (in Chapter Two) as hard skills, including technical and safety skills; soft skills, such as communication and facilitation; and meta skills, such as problem-solving and decision-making.

Because these qualities are often difficult to measure, and recognizing that even the best teachers are only human, it is also important for an organization to provide adequate education, supervision, and backup to instructors. Orientation and training programs can help clarify expectations, eliminate assumptions, and provide direction to new employees. Written parameters can supplement judgment and provide guidance, improving the chance that nothing will be forgotten. Supervision allows more-seasoned instructors to evaluate the skills of new employees in the field. Together, these measures improve an organization's ability to hire, develop, and retain "the best people."

In Chapter Seven, Conni Livsey and Bill Ennis discuss some of the challenges AOEE faced during its 25-year evolution in regard to instructor selection and hiring. As is common with many small organizations, in the early days of UAA's program, hiring decisions were usually based on the fact that the manager knew, had worked with, and trusted each instructor candidate. No one considered it necessary to write down hiring criteria or to have a formal interview process or apprenticeship program. The local climbing community was small, and the members knew each other well.

Over the years, the program grew, not only in number of students and instructors, but also in the scope of its ventures. In 1972, for instance, the department offered only a few courses (in mountaineering and survival), and employed only a handful of instructors. By 1992, the department offered more than 50 courses and included a staff of more than 40 adjunct faculty. During this transition, many of the more experienced instructors left, and less experienced or unknown employees were hired to replace them or to teach the new activities. As a result, it became difficult, if not impossible, for the program's manager to have intimate knowledge of each instructor's strengths and weaknesses, as well as to have a solid understanding of the skills and background needed for the wide range of courses offered. Because there was no formal process in place, the manager often had to make hiring decisions based on incomplete information.

Although the department began formalizing its system of selecting and training its instructors in the mid-1990s, the Ptarmigan Peak accident gave impetus to a more uniform approach to hiring new employees. We began by developing a comprehensive list of basic criteria that would be required of all new hires. We want all lead instructors to have a high degree of technical skills and personal experience; a background in leading or guiding groups of people; a background in teaching and facilitation; and current certification in medical and rescue skills. The list, which includes a variety of hard skills, soft skills, and meta skills, is included in Appendix B.

Now, instead of relying on who we know, we evaluate

candidates according to these criteria. We require and collect resumes and certifications. We use questionnaires to learn about a person's experience with local hazards and environmental conditions. Letters of recommendations from employers or outdoor professionals give us insight into the candidate's character and judgment in the field. Phone calls to references are made for the same purpose. With this multi-tiered and comprehensive approach, we get a more complete picture of each candidate's strengths and weaknesses.

Of course, hiring is only the first step of the process. Effective orientation, training, and evaluation are also critical aspects of an instructor's development. In order to address these important steps, AOEE adopted a modified approach to instructor training and evaluation.

AOEE field staff start their employment as assistant instructors (typically in lower-risk courses) with the knowledge that they will be evaluated by others. Every attempt is made to place them with strong leaders and more experienced instructors who can mentor them and provide them with unbiased feedback. Although there is no set timeline for promotion, by gathering information from a number of sources, the program manager can adequately assess the candidates' skill levels and competencies, and can therefore make an educated decision about whether or not they are qualified for continued employment or advancement.

Other organizations, like the National Outdoor Leadership School and Outward Bound, provide even more thorough instructor candidate trainings and/or field practicums for new hires. They may, for example, require new employees or instructor candidates to attend a multi-day training program that includes didactic and practical sessions. Often this is done prior to a new instructor being allowed to work in the field. In this way, potential or new instructors can be observed in a variety of settings and can be evaluated by a number of people. These training sessions also provide a great opportunity to educate a prospective hire about an agency's mission and risk management philosophy.

Although AOEE does not conduct a training program this extensive, we have implemented a new formal orientation for new employees that includes a discussion of the agency's mission statement, risk management goals and philosophy, and program policies and procedures. We believe that taking the time to verbally review these important concepts helps reinforce their importance and effectively instills clear expectations and program ideology from day one. The benefits of taking time to discuss these concepts with a new hire will outweigh the time that could be saved by simply handing a policy and procedure manual to an employee, asking him or her to read it, and then assuming the subjects are known and understood.

A final aspect of instructor training is continuing education to ensure that instructors stay current with their skills. Ongoing instructor training is expensive and time-consuming and can be a challenge for any organization, particularly for those that provide mostly seasonal or temporary employment. Nevertheless, it is important for instructors to maintain their training and continually hone their skills. A "rusty" group leader has the potential to be much more expensive to an organization than his current-but-costly counterpart.

A "rusty" group leader has the potential to be much more expensive to an organization than his current-but-costly counterpart.

Some programs have identified creative solutions, such as opening their trainings to members of the public or joining with another organization to minimize costs. Other groups offer raises to employees who complete applicable workshops through an outside source.

Our program has addressed this challenge by offering two to three in-house trainings each year, and by supplementing the cost of continued education on an ongoing basis. In 1999, for example, the department conducted field sessions in technical rescue methods as well as avalanche hazard evaluation and rescue skills. In 2000, we offered trainings in search and rescue, water safety, and river-crossing techniques. In our experience, it has been expensive and difficult to schedule the sessions, and rarely can everyone attend. Nevertheless, we believe that the more of this kind of training we can provide, the better equipped our instructors will be to provide safe, educational, and meaningful experiences for our students.

Volunteers

The use of unpaid (volunteer) staff is fairly common in

outdoor agencies. In fact, some programs run exclusively on volunteers or use a limited number of paid staff to supervise and support the volunteer crew.

Using volunteers can be an effective way of minimizing costs, and it can provide an excellent training ground for potential future employees. But it is not without risk. A volunteer, who is rarely held to the same hiring and training standards as an employee, cannot be expected to provide the same level of leadership, competence, or commitment as a paid instructor. Nor should volunteers be used to supplement instructor/student ratios.

Organizations that use volunteers on field outings should carefully evaluate what effect the practice has on their overall ability to manage risk.

Organizations that use volunteers on field outings should carefully evaluate what effect the practice has on their overall ability to manage risk. If your first reaction is "none," you'd be wise to think again. In the event of an accident, the practice is almost sure to be questioned, especially if a volunteer is being used in place of a paid instructor.

Prior to 1997, AOEE used volunteers in many of its classes. There were no written guidelines that described volunteer selection or training criteria. Further, there were no clearly defined policies regarding what a volunteer could and could not do in the field. To minimize the potential for problems in the future, we decided to create minimum "hiring" standards (which are similar to but not as high as those expected of an instructor) and to clarify the roles and expectations of volunteers used in courses. For instance, we expect our volunteers to have higher technical skills than the students. They must have at least a year of personal experience in the activity in which they'll be helping. They must "work" under the direct supervision of the lead or assistant instructors. And they are required to meet with the instructors before and after each outing in order to clarify roles and give/receive feedback. (For a complete listing of volunteer prerequisites and expectations, see Appendix C). Prior to entering the field, volunteers are also required to attend an orientation similar to that of a new paid employee.

By addressing this gray area, we have made it clear that AOEE volunteers are not expected to take the place of an instructor. Instead, volunteers provide an extra set of eyes and ears for the paid employees. And though the program has potentially minimized the usefulness of volunteer positions, we strive to make sure the relationship is mutually beneficial. The volunteer who is hoping to (and often does) become an assistant instructor is given an opportunity to learn AOEE's management philosophy and field practices. Instructors are able to observe and evaluate the volunteer's skills during outings. By incorporating more formality into this process, AOEE not only improved its risk management practices but also established a semi-formal apprenticeship program.

Students

Selecting the "right" participants for a course or trip is far more challenging than simply creating a flashy brochure and collecting registration information. The goal is to get a good fit between customer and activity, which means matching expectations to reality and physical ability to the demands of the field experience. When the fit is good, everyone is more likely to achieve his or her goals and walk away satisfied. When the fit is bad, it can lead to disaster.

Because promotional literature is usually designed to sell a course and attract new clients, the natural tendency is to pick the most exciting language and spectacular photographs, and to use the most enthusiastic endorsements from previous students. But ironically, there is risk in presenting a course in too good a light. Outdoor industry legal expert Reb Gregg cautions against using only pictures of smiling students in spectacular settings. This kind of advertising, he points out, can convey a false image of what the environment will be like and can create unrealistic expectations regarding the participants' comfort and well-being. After all, this is the outdoors. The weather can be quite challenging, to say the least, and not all trips end in success.

At the opposite extreme is advertising that is too negative. Literature that focuses only on difficult conditions and risk is not likely to attract any customers at all. Further, while an agency may be tempted to overrate the difficulty of a course to ensure that only suitable students apply, it may be setting itself up for trouble if it is too quick to judge those individuals who might appear unfit. Not only is it likely to turn away perfectly able students or clients, but it might end up getting an abrupt and unsolicited education about the Americans with Disabilities Act as well (see Chapter Four for more details).

A third approach to marketing is one that uses promotional literature to educate and inform. Brochures, catalogs, and course descriptions can help prepare students for the experiences they will encounter in the field and enable them to make knowledgeable decisions about whether a particular course is right for them. When an organization takes the time to inform potential customers about what they can expect, what challenges and risks they are likely to face, and what minimum skill and fitness levels are required for each activity, it does two important things: It increases the odds that there will be a good fit between customer and activity, and it reduces the number of under-prepared and unqualified people who end up in the field.

This idea of educating students so that they can make knowledgeable decisions regarding participation is known as informed consent. The legal benefits of properly informing clients are further addressed in Chapter Four, and the ethical considerations are discussed in Chapter Six. But it is valuable to note here that the practice can also aid in preventing accidents. Informed and educated participants are better equipped to recognize hazards and consequently can assist in risk assessment and management. Further, when an instructor does a good job educating group members about potential risk and the steps that can be used to minimize it, students are often more engaged and apt to accept some responsibility for their own and others' well-being.

In the previous section, we addressed the process of selecting activities that enhance an organization's mission and that can be safely administered within an organization's resources. The process of matching potential clients starts with a similar analysis. We can begin by creating a realistic portrait of the "ideal" person for each activity. First, look at the goals and objectives of the course. Second, think about baseline skills, fitness, and education levels that will be required to meet those objectives. Third, identify conditions —such as age, agility, and physical disabilities—that potentially could affect a participant's ability to successfully complete the course. And finally, consider whether or not reasonable accommodations can be made to compensate for each of those conditions. By taking these steps, you will have improved the odds that a good fit has been created and the course will be a success for all.

Once students or clients are enrolled, an agency can further minimize potential problems by learning about each participant's medical background and by helping them prepare (physically and mentally) for the outing. Instructors and managers alike need to know when their clients have pre-existing medical conditions, such as asthma, diabetes, or a seizure disorder. Some conditions may pose enough of a concern that a physician's advice will be needed. In a few cases, the student might not be allowed to participate (again, see Chapter Four). But often this information does not have to be used to prevent a student from engaging in an outing. By anticipating needs and helping educate the participant about what to expect, an agency can often prevent problems from developing. When medical needs or conditions are identified in advance, an organization has time to consider and plan for "what ifs," and to take whatever precautionary measures are necessary.

During UAA's year-long review process, we paid particular attention to these areas of marketing and student selection. Like most programs, we had always provided some course information to our students. However, when we looked more closely, we realized that our student population had changed significantly over the years and our marketing strategy had not. Consequently, we decided to try an altogether different approach in order to properly educate students and prepare them for the field.

Fifteen to 20 years ago, the majority of our students were what educators call "nontraditional." They were 25 years old or older, often held professional positions, and had already completed their higher education. They typically enrolled in our courses out of personal interest and hoped to master new skills. They were intent, focused, and heavily invested in what was being taught.

Gradually, the demographics changed, and by 1997 many courses were filled with 18- to 24-year-old, full-time "traditional" university students. Some were looking for an easy or interesting credit; others responded to our promotional literature and just wanted "to have fun." In either case, this type of student was not necessarily focused on or invested in the activity for its own sake. Further, because a greater percentage of the younger students were less familiar with the outdoors, it was common for them to be less efficient at recognizing risk or performing a risk-benefit analysis. When the department looked back at how the students in the 1970s and 1980s had been able to assimilate information and apply their life experiences to the classroom, we recognized how significantly this had affected their ability to make educated choices about risk. The younger students, with fewer life experiences upon which to draw, seemed less equipped to do the same. It became apparent that we needed to revise our techniques to be more effective with today's very different students.

As a result, the program changed its literature to more accurately describe what a student might expect. The following example is a quote listed in the UAA catalog:

> *Many of AOEE's classes are held in Alaska's wilderness, an environment that can pose a risk to even the most experienced outdoor leader. Students may be required to perform activities in extremely inclement weather; i.e., rain, sleet, snow, wind or sub-zero temperatures.*

Additional catalog information identifies minimum fitness levels and venue/terrain difficulty. Further, the catalog and brochures note that students will be asked to sign acknowledgement of risk, release of liability, and medical questionnaire forms. This information allows prospective participants to screen themselves and make informed choices about whether or not a course is right for them. Often, if students think they are unfit, unqualified, or unprepared, they choose not to enroll.

We also spend more energy helping our novice and younger students understand the actual (vs. perceived) risks involved in each activity. Risk Recognition and Risk-Benefit Analysis are now required subjects in all our courses. Instructors are required to clearly explain and discuss the new acknowledgement of risk forms. Some instructors revisit these topics halfway through a semester. They may even have students re-sign the forms after they have a better understanding of the inherent risks associated with the activity and can make a more educated decision about whether or not they want to continue.

Although most of the work identified here is done with the goal of increasing student satisfaction and preventing accidents, it is worth noting that when we document our actions, we are also helping to protect ourselves in the event an incident does occur (see Chapter Four). Prior to any outing, all paperwork associated with risk management should be collected and stored in a secure but accessible location.

Venues used in professional settings, particularly those that serve beginning or inexperienced clients, should always be selected with careful attention to the risk factors.

WHERE: Venue Selection

Venue selection is one of the most frequently overlooked aspects of a risk management plan. Too often, organizations choose venues based on a particular site's popularity or marketability instead of thoroughly assessing its attendant risks. At times, venues are used to satisfy an instructor's agenda. However, as Jasper Hunt points out in Chapter Six, it is unacceptable for instructors, bored with the "easy and familiar" routes, to take clients to more challenging venues simply for personal pleasure. Although they may convince themselves that the experience will benefit all, the choice may also increase the level of risk to students unnecessarily. Venues used in professional settings, particularly those that serve beginning or inexperienced clients, should always be selected with careful attention to the risk factors.

Realistically, an agency will consider a number of factors (including cost, convenience, and marketability) when it is deciding which venues to use. However, the final decision should be based on considerations already identified in this chapter: the program's mission; the hazards associated with the area; the experience, skill level, and readiness of the students and instructors; and the goals of the activity. Does the site provide the type of terrain necessary to meet course goals? Can the course goals be met by using another, less-hazardous site? Are there good teaching spots or enough camping locations in the area? Once these details have been considered, an organization can feel confident that the decision was made with course success and participant safety in mind.

To illustrate how this process can work, consider the following example from AOEE's recent history. Our department used to offer a backcountry skiing course in the Ruth Amphitheater, a natural and spectacular feature of the Alaska Range. The setting, which can be reached only by a small ski plane, was the main draw of the course. However, the terrain was glacial and crevasses were commonplace. The weather was unpredictable, and groups could be stranded for days at a time, far beyond the reach of emergency assistance.

In order to prepare students properly for the hazards of this setting, we realized we would have to devote significantly more time to student readiness. Several days would need to be added to the course in order to cover the fundamental information. We couldn't help wondering if we'd be better off finding a more suitable location, one that provided a better fit for beginning students and course goals. During the review process, we discussed changing the location but keeping the outline, modifying and lengthening the course, or dropping the class entirely. We chose the first option, and we now offer Skiing Alaska's Backcountry in less spectacular, but still beautiful, terrain. The new course area is more conducive to teaching beginning backcountry ski skills, and the risks are much more appropriate for the inexperienced student.

We applied this same kind of process to decide which venues would be used in all our courses. Using the criteria listed below, we ultimately approved more than 80 separate sites and wrote comprehensive guides for each. Each course has roughly a dozen approved venues from which an instructor can choose. This system allows us to provide course leaders with a certain amount of variability and freedom within a managed framework.

The following is a list of considerations we use in our venue-selection process:

- Venues should promote a program's mission statement and be appropriate for course or activity goals and objectives while minimizing risk to participants.
- Venues (especially those being used by beginning or inexperienced clients) should never be used as a reconnais-

sance (often referred to as "recon") or to satisfy an instructor's personal agenda.

- Venues should be within the skill/fitness level of all participants.
- Venues should be free of unnecessary hazards. Venues that have not been visited for a while should be scouted before the outing. If possible, minimize or eliminate unnecessary hazards (e.g., rockfall or river debris) prior to the outing.
- Remote sites increase the consequences in the event of an accident or emergency. Therefore, if a remote site is chosen, more intense risk management steps should be taken, lower-risk activities should be chosen, and more conservative decisions should be made.
- Sites should be studied (and visited if possible) in a variety of seasons and conditions. Hazards should be identified and weather patterns noted.
- Venues should have primary routes and secondary or contingency routes. Each area should always have an escape route or option in the event that unfavorable conditions (weather, high water or avalanche hazard, for example) do not allow safe travel, escape, or descent on the main route.
- The program manager and instructors should have an agreed-upon plan regarding course options in the event a route does not allow safe travel. Instructors should recognize that there are times when it is best to select an alternate route or even turn a group around. If options have not been pre-approved or discussed ahead of time, instructors might feel compelled to continue.
- Once an area is selected and approved, a venue guide should be developed. The venue guide should include, but not be limited to, identification of known hazards, routes, and contingency routes; typical weather and weather patterns; water; camping; times and distances; and nearest phone and/or emergency services. Instructors should be familiar with the information provided in the venue guide.
- Students should be informed of inherent risks and educated about risk-management steps that will be used by the program. If there is a chance a hazard will be faced in that venue (e.g., a river must be crossed), students must be educated about the proper steps needed to recognize, mini-

mize and possibly encounter the risk. They should also be trained in how to deal with field emergencies associated with the hazard. (I once observed a group doing a fabulous job of teaching students how to properly cross a stream or river. Unfortunately, the members had never been told what to do if any of them "went for a swim.")

- The program should consider the environmental impact that student groups will have on an area.
- Land managers should be contacted for any additional information about site considerations, all necessary permits (or permission) must be obtained, and a trip plan (and emergency information) should be left with appropriate personnel.

If there is ever a question about whether or not a given site or route is appropriate for a group, an instructor should remember why they are there and consider the whole group's well-being. If these conditions are ever compromised, instructors should be ready and willing to change their route or plans.

WHEN: Scheduling

Deciding when to schedule an outing may take nothing more than a few minutes of thought. Nonetheless, at least two issues should be considered before the dates are confirmed: environmental factors and resource availability, as each relates to risk management. While the first consideration is commonly and appropriately addressed by most organizations, the second can be problematic for many outdoor agencies. These factors are important enough that they are worth exploring further.

No matter where an organization operates, there will be a higher likelihood of facing certain environmental hazards at given times of the year. Rivers may be high in June, snow bridges weak in May, or snow loads predictably unstable in January. Ultimately, if an outing occurs during poor field conditions, the group's ability to meet its course and risk management goals can be greatly affected. As a result, even though a venue is appropriate with respect to course objectives and personnel, the area might be unsuitable for use during a certain time of year (due to environmental conditions). Keep in mind, the timing and conditions don't need to change much to provide an entirely different scene (e.g., don't be surprised when the field of flowers where you camped in June is still filled with snow in May). By gathering reliable information about local environmental and weather conditions, an agency can maximize the chance that a group will be able to avoid predictable hazards, or at least be prepared for a possible encounter.

A second scheduling issue, one that AOEE and other outdoor programs around the country seem to be facing, is the shortage of experienced outdoor instructors to lead courses. Many program managers have said that more and more of their instructor candidates are applying with less and less field and leadership experience. This is not to say that they are unqualified, but because the information used to assess candidates is changing (extensive personal and professional experience is often being replaced with formal classroom training or a more-structured outing background), managers are forced to make decisions based on paper credentials and certifications rather than proven experience and judgment.

When multiple courses are scheduled concurrently, or when a course is scheduled and an instructor becomes ill or injured at the last minute, it can be difficult to find a qualified replacement, especially on short notice. Consequently, a manager may be faced with the difficult choice between canceling a course or using an untested employee. If the instructor candidate is obviously inexperienced, the decision can be easy. But when the candidate looks strong on paper, and the program director is under pressure to make money, the decision is not always black and white. In times like these, an assistant may be quickly upgraded or an unknown instructor hired to fill the slot, even though risk management ultimately may be unintentionally compromised as a result.

Instructors aren't the only resource that can be in short supply. Another problem associated with scheduling concurrent trips is a lack of adequate supplies. Although an organization usually has requirements about the equipment that must be taken on an outing, if students show up with inadequate gear, if equipment is lost or damaged during a trip, or if courses are scheduled with the assumption that they won't all "go," there is potential for problems. As a result, people may end up in the field without proper group, personal, or safety gear.

Because agencies often must plan their outings in advance, and because it is difficult to know which courses will fill and which instructors will be available, it is not always realistic to totally avoid overlap in a schedule. But at minimum, schedulers should consider the consequences of all courses filling, an instructor becoming unavailable, or a strong-looking applicant not meeting minimum performance standards. Just as contingency plans are made in the event of field emergencies, a contingency plan for lack of equipment or qualified staff should be made long before a crisis arises.

Policies and rules are not the enemy; they can be used to guide an instructor's decisions and minimize risk.

HOW: Accepted Field Practices

So far this chapter has identified potential problems that can be handled before an outing begins. These concerns, typically addressed by managers and administrators, have to do with program philosophy, selection and training of staff and students, and choice of venue. This section discusses risk management considerations that are more directly shared by group leaders and instructors.

Many organizations choose to limit the number of policies field staff must follow, leaving it up to the instructor to decide exactly how a course is run. While this approach has its supporters, it is probably neither the safest nor the best way to run an operation. Policies and rules are not the enemy; they can be used to guide an instructor's decisions and minimize risk.

Identifying accepted field practice is no different than adopting a particular system for the hiring and training of staff. The goal is to ensure that appropriate decisions are made based on agreed-upon criteria rather than individual whim. By scripting the protocols and having them available for instructor and student reference, an organization can minimize assumptions, provide clarification and expectations, and create backup systems to make sure nothing important is forgotten.

Outdoor leaders sometimes object that too many policies interfere with instructor judgment. But a policy is not a step-by-step set of orders, designed to minimize an instructor's ability to think. Instead, it is a course of action, arrived at after considerable debate, that an organization adopts to help it achieve its goals. For example, an organization may identify as policy the practice of wearing helmets while ice climbing. Instructors are expected to comply with this rule under all normal circumstances, because the organization has determined that this is the best course of action in nearly every case. But while the policy limits an instructor's decisions about the wearing of helmets, it does not try to tell him how to teach the class.

When writing policy, it is helpful to get input from a variety of people, perhaps even a risk management committee. A policy should reflect the program's mission and philosophy. It should also make sense—to administrators, trip leaders, and students. And once a policy has been identified, it is important that people at all levels of the organization know it, accept it, and understand that they are expected to follow it.

During AOEE's review, all field techniques were thoroughly scrutinized by a newly instituted Risk Management Advisory Committee (RMAC). By first identifying the risks inherent in each activity, we were able to address common dangers and craft policies that outlined accepted field practices. We also addressed and tried to minimize some of the risks more generically associated with any backcountry course, such as avoiding or dealing with animal encounters. Although many of the new policies were not directly associated with the Ptarmigan Peak accident, by searching for potential weaknesses in our risk management system we were able to identify many areas that could ultimately be improved. Below are some examples of AOEE's new policies and the thought process that went into creating them.

Equipment

If we're going to supply equipment during a course, we reasoned, we need to have a system in place to ensure that the gear is appropriately distributed, adequately maintained, and properly stored. AOEE has instituted a computerized inventory system and is currently able to track items that are used in its courses. An equipment room manager is responsible for gear maintenance. These changes have resulted in a dramatic decrease in the amount of stolen and lost gear as well as the number of times damaged equipment inadvertently ends up in the field.

AOEE has also improved how it monitors student equipment. In the classroom, we have always provided students with equipment lists so that they know what to bring on outings. Unfortunately, gear lists alone do not guarantee that all items make it into the field. Our instructors have often been frustrated when students fail to bring everything on the lists, but the solutions sometimes seemed as frustrating as the problem. While it is essential for students to have appropriate gear, comprehensive gear checks consume a significant percentage of class time (especially when one considers that most of our outings last a weekend). Part of our mission is to educate students so that they develop the knowledge and experience necessary to participate in an activity outside of a formal and supervised class. Although we recognize that some type of check must be used, continuing the practice of requiring full gear checks on the fifth or sixth outing did not seem to support course goals of self-sufficiency and personal responsibility.

As a compromise, we developed a procedure for identifying essential items for each course that must be carried on all trips. The individual lists are not as extensive as the full-course inventories that were previously recommended, but each directory includes equipment that is considered necessary for a student's safety and survival. At minimum, every person (or every group if the outing is a day trip) is required to carry survival equipment, first aid and repair supplies, and a communication or signaling device. In certain courses, such as mountaineering, the list is expanded and includes items such as a helmet, ice axe, beacon, shovel, and a probe. Further, AOEE policy now states that a "parking lot" check is required to verify that all of the essential items identified above are carried into the field. Instructors can use their discretion to decide if or when full gear checks are needed. This system is less time-consuming and places some responsibility on the student, but it is also very helpful in ensuring that irreplaceable gear is not left behind.

Transportation

Any agency that transfers clients to or from an outing site (by vehicle, boat, or plane) should consider setting policy for its transportation practices. Agencies that do not provide transportation but allow participants to use their own vehicles may want to set policy too; surprisingly, this practice can be a legal gray area in the event of an accident. Additional problems can occur if an accident happens when the transport is conducted by someone other than the outdoor organization (for instance, when a group hires a boat to get across a bay, or when students use local transportation in a foreign country).

At minimum, it is important to talk to students about the risks associated with transportation and to incorporate these hazards into an agency's acknowledgement of risk and release forms. But there are also ways to minimize the risks themselves. If the agency uses its own vehicle, for instance, it is wise to create a system that clearly tracks the vehicle's maintenance. Drivers should be properly trained regarding vehicle use, driver histories should be obtained, and each driver should be able to locate and use emergency equipment.

An additional step AOEE now takes is to clearly identify when an outing starts and ends. By advising students that they are responsible for getting to and from a trailhead, AOEE has minimized the legal quagmire that can occur when a student runs into trouble on the road. Further, the department only makes flight or boat transport arrangements with companies that are insured and can provide maintenance records. By taking these steps, an agency can enhance its risk management practices while limiting its legal liability exposure.

Pilots, though highly trained, rely heavily on checklists, and outdoor leaders would do well to follow their example.

Checklists, Buddy Checks, and Safety Briefings

Pilots, though highly trained, rely heavily on checklists, and outdoor leaders would do well to follow their example. Checklists are an excellent way to ensure that essential steps are not overlooked or items forgotten. AOEE now includes a checklist in the front of each instructor field manual. These lists reminds instructors to:

- ✓Check for essential equipment (including first aid kit, trauma kit, repair supplies, and bear spray)
- ✓Check the live weather forecast
- ✓Review the venue guide for the outing
- ✓Go over the lost person protocol and animal encounter policies with students

✓Meet with co-instructors regarding roles and expectations
✓Give a safety talk to students before heading out, and
✓Call the AOEE office as soon as the group is out of the field at the end of the trip

Other department policies require backups and buddy checks as standard operating procedure on virtually all our activities. For example, just as buddy checks are conducted to see that carabiners are locked and harnesses are doubled back, instructors are also required to check each other's work whenever safety is involved. Groups are required to adhere to a buddy system during travel, and all participants are expected to continually check the physical and emotional well-being of their partners. A safety briefing must be conducted before every outing, and the checklist reminds groups to discuss potential hazards before they enter the field. Not only can these practices catch potential errors or oversights, they are a good way to model risk management behaviors and let students see that their instructors use backup systems even though they are experienced professionals.

Solo Instruction

Solo instructing is a somewhat controversial practice in the outdoor industry. If group size is small, and if an instructor is able to supervise all members and provide quality leadership without the aid of an assistant, an agency may choose to allow an instructor to work alone. Although legitimate arguments can be made for and against the practice, many factors should be considered before it is allowed.

In part, the decision should be based on an organization's mission, the activity, the course objectives, the experience level of the group, and the risk involved. It is common for organizations to practice solo instructing on natural history walks, for instance. Further, if students are fairly competent and could help in an emergency, and if one of the group's goals is to develop self-sufficiency in members, the practice of solo instructing might be justified.

If group members are inexperienced, however, and a solo instructor becomes incapacitated, the consequences could be very serious and detrimental to the group's (as well as the instructor's) well-being. This is an especially critical consideration if a group will be traveling in technical or remote terrain or if novice students would be required to provide or find help.

Because of the concerns associated with the practice, AOEE does not allow instructors to work alone outside the Anchorage city limits. If an organization decides to allow solo instructing, however, it should take steps to minimize the increased risk that the practice creates. A group with a single instructor should consider conducting relatively low-risk (non-technical) activities, traveling in less-hazardous terrain, and making more conservative decisions. Further, the organization may choose to set up a communication system through which the instructor is able to check in at specified intervals. Finally, any agency that allows solo instructing should be ready—with students trained and prepared—in the event an instructor becomes incapacitated in the field.

Solo Travel

Like many organizations, AOEE encourages its instructors and students to use the buddy system as standard practice. There are times, however, when an agency might find it tempting or even necessary to deviate from this practice and allow solo travel. Such instances might arise when someone needs to join an outing after it has started or leave before it has finished, when a supervisor or course director hikes in to check on a team, or when an instructor or assistant escorts a student out of the field and then returns to the group alone.

In some cases (such as glacier travel or on technical terrain), the act of solo travel itself is so hazardous it can easily be ruled out. In many other cases, however, it is not the travel that causes the greatest concern; instead, it is the potential consequence if something goes wrong and the solo traveler is unable to summon help.

The decision to allow solo travel should never be made casually, or for the sake of convenience or money. Instead, organizations need to thoroughly examine their reasons and carefully weigh the benefits and risks. An agency that allows the practice must be prepared to justify it, to explain how the practice contributes to the program's mission and course outcomes.

The decision-making process should include contingency planning as well, including an examination of the "what ifs" in the event something goes wrong. The solo traveler should be prepared in the event he becomes lost or injured. At minimum, this means informing others of the intended route (similar to filing a flight plan), estimating a time of arrival, and carrying survival equipment as well as a signaling device and/or cell phone in case of an emergency. Organizations and groups should also be prepared with a pre-arranged search and rescue strategy if the traveler does not arrive at his destination on time.

The decision to allow solo travel should never be made casually, or for the sake of convenience or money.

After considering all these factors, our risk management committee could think of no circumstance that would necessitate solo travel in our courses. Consequently, the practice is forbidden on AOEE outings. On out-of-town trips, teams travel in groups of six or more, and at least two instructors are always in attendance. AOEE participants are not allowed to join a group after it has left the trailhead, and participants cannot leave an outing early except in an emergency. In the event of an accident that requires someone to go for help, runner teams are used.

In fact, AOEE groups are not expected to separate. Realizing, however, that a team of two could conceivably and appropriately want or need to be apart from the main group for a short period of time, the committee examined potential exceptions to the rule, and policy was created to offer guidance. For example, in extenuating circumstances, people can arrange to join a group late or depart early as long as they use the buddy system and make prearranged contingency and communication plans. The same setup is used when participants want to take an evening walk or need to spend time away from the group.

Lost Person Policies

Although AOEE had experienced some close calls through the years with students becoming separated from their groups, it was only during our comprehensive review process that we recognized the importance of having a formal lost person policy. Prior to 1997, this potential hazard was not routinely addressed with students, and instructors had seldom educated group members on what to do if they became lost.

Our advisory committee sought input from search-and-rescue experts to learn which steps would most likely affect (positively or negatively) a missing-person situation. First and foremost, we learned, is the importance of timing. The first hour is critical in finding a missing person, and search procedures need to be immediate and efficient if they are to succeed. Considering the venues we typically use, if the lost person can't be found within a very short period of time, we decided it would be wise to seek outside help as quickly as possible. Delays can be deadly.

AOEE now requires instructors and students to review the department's lost person policy at the start of every trip. Before entering the field, participants are reminded to be aware of their surroundings, use the buddy system, and avoid becoming separated from the group. If they do become separated, students are instructed to make noise, leave clues, and refrain from wandering even deeper into the terrain. The group discusses its own course of action, how it will initiate a search, and if conditions are hazardous or the initial brief search is unsuccessful, how it will dispatch a runner team to seek outside assistance. The group also acknowledges the fact that the instructor might be the one who becomes lost. Ultimately, by acknowledging the potential danger and being prepared, we have taken positive steps in minimizing the possibility of an accident before it has the chance to develop.

Animal/Human Encounters

Every outdoor agency needs to think about the potential for unwanted animal or human interactions that might occur during a course. What small or large animals, reptiles, or insects live in the area that can become a nuisance or a threat? Are vandals known to frequent the region? Will the group be crossing or traveling close to any private property? What can be done to avoid or deal with each of these encounters? While it may not be practical to prepare students for every conceivable encounter, it is worthwhile to teach them about the potential dangers associated with an area. Sometimes the less evident hazards become the more troublesome problems, often because group members are not able to recognize the threat before it is too late.

In Alaska, for example, "bear talks" are included in most pre-trip training sessions given by outdoor leaders. Students and visitors are taught to make noise in the back-country, hike in groups, keep a clean camp, and avoid surprising a bear. If an encounter does occur, people are advised to hold their ground, look big, wave their arms, and never run. When an attack seems imminent, conventional wisdom says a victim should get into a fetal position and play dead.

Interestingly, a different hazard that can be just as deadly is frequently ignored. Moose are much more common than bears and much more likely to be encountered by locals and visitors alike. Nonetheless, they are rarely even acknowledged by Alaskan guides and outdoor educators. A bear encounter may seem far more dramatic and terrifying, but it is a mistake to discount the likelihood and seriousness of running into a 1,000 pound moose.

After realizing we had overlooked the obvious, AOEE added "moose encounters" to "bear talks" as part of our pre-trip safety briefing. Before any group enters the field, instructors discuss the potential dangers of encountering bear and moose. Students are now reminded to keep their distance from both and not be complacent around either. They learn to recognize behaviors, such as head down and ears back and flat, that mean the moose is unhappy. And they learn what to do in the event of an attack: hide behind a tree, use pepper spray, or get out of the way.

Environmental Hazards

In many AOEE courses, there are times when objective hazards, such as river crossings and avalanche terrain, cannot be avoided. Although instructors have always been required to train students in the recognition and minimization of these risks, we had few policies that would clearly identify "dos and don'ts" to guide our instructors. Our risk management committee believed it was important to address these high-risk situations and identify some "always and never" rules that could be used to supplement instructor judgment and training. Again, the rules don't tell the instructor how something must be done (like crossing a river), but they do note that students must have at least a minimal level of training before attempting a crossing, and they must be educated in the event something goes wrong. An example of one such policy for traveling in avalanche terrain is included in Appendix D. The policy identifies slopes that AOEE considers potentially hazardous, instructor and participant training that we require, and safety equipment we consider essential (e.g., a beacon, a shovel, a probe and an inclinometer).

It is impossible to use policies to completely ensure that a river or snow-slope crossing is carried out safely; the ultimate decision of whether or not to cross remains in the hands of the instructor. Yet an agency can specify certain precautionary measures an instructor must take and can identify preferred methods, always with the understanding that the final choice will be dependent on the conditions.

No policy can guarantee safety; however, it is important to remember that policies, such as those identified throughout this section, have a place in a risk management plan. Not only can they be used as effective tools for modeling and reinforcing good habits, but if designed carefully and practiced regularly, they can enhance the overall quality of an agency's risk management system.

Implementing and Maintaining the Plan

Creating a well-thought-out risk management plan is a time-consuming process, but an agency's work does not end there. Once a plan has been crafted, it must also be implemented and maintained. It is extremely helpful to have a designated risk manager to ensure that all tasks are accomplished and details of the plan are not overlooked. This manager—often the organization's owner or director—must make sure that all aspects of the plan have been considered and addressed. He or she may delegate various aspects of implementation and oversight to other people or to a committee, but ultimately the manager is responsible for ensuring that everything is in place.

AOEE's program coordinator has always held the role of risk manager for the department. However, the procedure for maintaining the program's risk management plan has been modified to include more active involvement from course instructors as well as the advisory committee (RMAC). The risk manager is still responsible for implementing changes, but she is not free to simply impose rules at her discretion. Before any changes are made, instructors provide input and the RMAC makes recommendations. If the coordinator rejects a committee recommendation, the college's dean becomes involved. In fact, the RMAC now plays an integral role in providing ongoing oversight in the upkeep of the plan. The group, which is a mixture of community experts and AOEE faculty, is responsible for reviewing field and hiring policies, course curriculum, venue guides, and accident or close-call reports on a regular basis.

A low accident rate is just one measure of an organization's risk management strategy; it only looks backward, never forward.

The Evaluation Process

Ongoing evaluation is critical to the health of a program and its risk management plan. As earlier chapters noted, it is important for an agency to realize that being accident-free does not mean it is doing everything right. A low accident rate is just one measure of an organization's risk management strategy; it only looks backward, never forward. To get the complete picture, an organization must continually assess and reassess its operation, keeping in mind its own evolution and changes that are going on in the industry at large.

Evaluations are a common part of most outdoor programs, but many times they are used simply to assess participant satisfaction. Rarely do they provide a true reflection of how well a program manages risk, how well the students were informed and prepared prior to the start of a course, or how sensitive an instructor was to his own and others' well-being.

Acknowledging these potential weaknesses, AOEE set about to improve our evaluation process. We started by encouraging an atmosphere of open communication and questioning. We also recognized that there are various levels of evaluations, so we created separate methods for assessing employees and courses.

In order to receive an assortment of data, AOEE now gathers input from a number of sources. The coordinator and staff evaluate one another, instructors and assistants do the same, and students and instructors give input on each other's strengths and weaknesses. Additionally, students are asked for feedback specific to risk management. The coordinator conducts site visits to offer input on instructors and courses. And advisory committee members take part in outings to assess field practices. Examples of the type of questions we use in our evaluation process are included in Appendix E. By adding these components to our process, we believe we have greatly improved how we critically assess our entire program.

Nevertheless, we recognize that with the exception of a few members of the RMAC, most of our student and staff feedback is internal and may not provide an unbiased evaluation of the risk management plan itself. Some organizations, like Outward Bound, have done an outstanding job of setting up systems for both internal and external professionals to conduct cyclic program reviews. Although we have not been able to arrange reviews quite as extensive as Outward Bound's, we do schedule cyclic peer and external reviews and advocate for the benefits they provide. In addition to offering new ideas, external reviewers can often see flaws that go unnoticed by members of the agency. A more comprehensive evaluation by peer reviewers or other professionals can be incredibly helpful to a program and should be an expected part of any agency's evaluation process.

Finally, in the event that some part of the risk management strategy does not work as planned and an incident or accident occurs, an organization should be prepared to investigate what went wrong and should be willing to critically evaluate its system. Much can be learned from accidents and incidents, and the investigation should be carried out with the intention that answers will lead to improvement rather than condemnation.

Long before they are ever faced with an actual real-life incident, organizations need to agree on which types of close calls and accidents will be investigated and how those investigations will be conducted. Steps to create or improve a crisis response plan are discussed elsewhere in this publication. Additionally, Jed Williamson's *Serious Incident/Accident Review Process* (1995) is included in Appendix F.

The importance of this issue cannot be overstated. It is basic to identify the events and factors that contributed to an accident, and it is essential that an organization use the information to make improvements wherever possible. Further, it is critical for organizations that function under the umbrella of a larger institution to communicate with the parent group to ensure that their crisis response and accident investigation plans are compatible. If an accident does occur, poor planning and faulty communication will add unnecessary stress and chaos, making a bad situation even worse.

Summary

The Alaska Outdoor & Experiential Education department and university community have learned a great deal since the Ptarmigan Peak accident, not only about the specifics of the fall itself, but also about how accidents generally tend to happen, how to be better prepared in the event a serious injury or fatality occurs, and what can be done to learn from and move beyond such a tragedy.

We have also learned that, as it is with accidents themselves, there is rarely a single cause that triggers system failure. Instead, a number of factors typically play a role. Although the university's outdoor program had not experienced a serious accident in many years, it seems that the department's risk management plan had not kept pace with the growth and evolution of the program itself. As would be the case with any small organization, practices that work well with only a few employees will likely be less effective when used in an agency 10 times its size. By thoroughly scrutinizing every aspect of our risk management plan—including but also going beyond those associated with the accident—we were able to identify and correct some of our weaknesses and build on our strengths. Ultimately, the program is stronger, students are given a higher quality education, and the risks are managed better than ever before.

It doesn't matter whether an agency is new or established, growing or status quo, even whether it is accident-free or not. No one is immune to change, and everyone can benefit from careful planning and on-going evaluation. Much progress has been made in the outdoor industry in the past 10 years. Risk management practices have improved and the standards have evolved. A program that doesn't recognize change or neglects to examine itself critically on a regular basis is simply asking for trouble. Accidents can happen to any of us, and it is in all our best interests to look closely at what we are doing and how we are doing it. Assessment is not about finding flaws: It is an indispensable tool for improvement.

Finally, we have a lot to learn from each other, both from things that have been done well and from mistakes that have been made. Hopefully the lessons uncovered as a result of the Ptarmigan Peak accident of 1997 and the review process that followed will never be lost. If these lessons can be helpful to program managers, practitioners, and students of outdoor education, the industry as a whole will have benefited and the tragedy will not have been in vain.

Assessment is not about finding flaws: It is an indispensable tool for improvement.

The Jury's In:

A Defense Lawyer's Perspective on Risk Management and Crisis Response

By R. Eldridge Hicks © 2000
with an addendum by Charles (Reb) Gregg

This chapter offers practical information on how to minimize legal liability in the presence of inherent risk. The author presents a variety of risk management and incident management strategies that demonstrate a pattern of conscientious compliance with community standards of care. The chapter concludes with an addendum by attorney Reb Gregg who examines the positive and negative aspects of open communication and investigation after an accident. Careful planning, such as the steps provided here, can help prevent accidents, and may also limit or prevent litigation if an accident does occur.

Ladies and Gentlemen of the Jury:

It is now up to you to decide whether or not Rachel violated the community standards of care among instructors and guides and if she must answer personally for the unfortunate death of Kevin.

We're not here to downplay that tragic death. A very good man died, and far too young. We're not asking you to find excuses for anyone or for anything. We don't want to minimize the heartache and pain this loss has brought to Kevin's family, his friends—and yes, to Rachel, too.

However, let's not forget that Kevin was engaging in an activity that has inherent risks. Remember how careful Rachel was to identify and point out those risks. Think about how those risks were managed and minimized by the anguished woman you judge today.

Recall, if you will, her teaching values. She testified that she treats students as she would her own family, because each of them is just that dear to someone out there. No lawyer put those words in her mouth. Long before this accident occurred, she wrote that precept at the top of her lesson plans and in her field notebook to remind herself repeatedly of her personal standard of care. Does that sound like a "negligent" woman?

Remember how thoroughly she assessed her clients for medical problems? She also assessed human shortcomings in them, as a standard practice. She made allowances for special needs, and she counseled them against errant behavior, such as machismo, inattentiveness, and other dangerous traits.

Think about the notes Rachel made in Kevin's folder, Exhibit D: "Eager but cautious ... coordinated, but not athletic … seems well organized … occasionally distracted by attentions from Kim." These entries are written in three different inks, demonstrating how she constantly added new information as she learned his behavior and needs. She made a point of knowing Kevin for one simple reason: so that she could be the very best possible guardian for him during his course.

Exhibit G is Rachel's detailed field plan and schedule. Read it together with Exhibit H, her field notebook. Skill-development exercises were carried out in the field, in perfect timing, in a precisely planned order, and always with a contingency plan available. As you review these documents, ask yourself whether a negligent person develops plans with this level of purpose and precision.

Consider also her regular attendance at continuing education seminars and workshops for instructors. She searched diligently to identify and meet the standards of her colleagues (as you see in Exhibit I). She developed safe training techniques and analyzed the accidents of others to learn how to avoid the same pitfalls. Her physical training regimen for the past four years is included in Exhibit J. Look at her. No one retains that level of fitness at age 42 without regular exercise.

You can read the entire professional history of Rachel as a guide and instructor in Exhibits K, L, M and N. In

Exhibits O, P, Q, R and S, you will find her wall calendar with tickler dates for gear inspections, repair logs going back three years, progress reports for every student, medical questionnaires, and releases, including the release where Kevin gave his informed, voluntary consent to take personal responsibility for the inherent risks of this adventure.

My colleague [gesture to plaintiff's counsel] questions whether a new student can ever give informed consent to risks not yet learned. Rachel agrees with him. That's why she spent half an hour outlining the activity's hazards and safety techniques before she even discussed the release with Kevin. That's why she asked him to repeat his consent with dated initials on two later occasions, as he learned more about the inherent risks. Kevin was never under any pressure to sign this simple document. He never suggested that he couldn't understand the plain English and bold type that indicated important terms.

Finally, how did Rachel respond to the accident? She was a cool, precise leader during the response and recovery effort. Then she went home and broke down completely. She attended grief therapy sessions for six weeks. With great sensitivity, she contacted Kevin's cousin to see if the family minded her coming to the memorial service. She came and she cried. She embraced Kevin's mother and assured Kevin's father that his questions would be answered, that we would learn the causes of the accident and report back to him. She stayed in touch. She showed compassion. Guilty, neglectful people don't act that way.

Ladies and gentlemen, please, allow for the very real possibility that despite the best-laid plans, people sometimes die. And death can come without one or more people being pointedly "to blame." That's all we ask …

Suddenly I lurched upright. "What's that buzzing noise? Where's the jury? Where's Rachel? The judge?"

I slapped the alarm clock, cleared the cobwebs, showered quickly, dressed while gulping coffee, and rushed away to an early morning oral argument in court—in the "real world" of defending personal injury cases. Unfortunately, in the real world, the facts for the defense are not always as perfect as they are in my dreams. Most defendants are not as together and presentable as Rachel, even if their intentions and goals are just as sincere and noble.

On my way to the office, in the bumper-to-bumper traffic, I asked myself, "What can I do to help people in the real world be more like the ones in my dreams? How can I convince them to take the steps now that will help me defend them later? What do I really wish was different in risk management and incident management for outdoor and adventure activities?

This chapter provides an answer of sorts. It examines several measures that can minimize two closely related risks in outdoor adventure programming: the risk of harm to the participant and the risk of negligence to the provider. By reviewing common mistakes and misperceptions that are made by outdoor adventure agencies, readers can improve their risk management and crisis response plans, especially in regard to legal liability exposure.

Why Should You Care?

As an outdoor leader or program administrator, you may be asking yourself, "Why should I care about legal liability?" You already know what you're going to do if something goes wrong: you'll say "no comment," and hire an attorney. Besides, you've got a million dollars worth of liability insurance coverage and very few personal assets. Or, perhaps the organization you work for has you covered. You're in good hands ... right?

Sorry. Neither a good lawyer nor the best insurance company in the world can cover you or protect you from the true costs associated with an accident. No insurance company, employer, or lawyer can shelter an accused defendant from the heartache, humiliation, and scrutiny of wrongful death litigation. Friends may betray you, there may be years of nagging emotional distractions, and no self-respecting person, no matter how innocent, stands up well against the sobbing, shrieking accusation "you killed my husband!"

You don't know true humiliation until you've been

grilled for two days by an attorney whose goal is to prove that you "willfully, wantonly, and maliciously" violated your duty of care to the young man with so much promise or the pretty young woman who left behind such an adorable baby girl. The attorney will confront you with every mistake and omission discoverable in your entire teaching or guiding career. Your perception of the "facts" will be construed and distorted so that you appear to be the most malicious, inept ogre in the industry. You will walk through the law office of opposing counsel knowing that the staff is staring at someone they consider "the killer." Nothing can shield you against such scrutiny and pain.

Neither a good lawyer nor the best insurance company in the world can cover you or protect you from the true costs associated with an accident.

If you are involved in an accident, you will also learn about true friends and loyalties. You will be shocked and mortified when a trusted old teaching colleague appears as an expert witness for the plaintiff. A guileless peer from a different agency might talk glibly, in damaging abstract terms, to an investigator hired by the plaintiff's attorney. Ex-employees or dissatisfied students may seek revenge by going to plaintiff's counsel with stories about careless maintenance practices (one time, many years ago) or examples of perceived disorganization, missed deadlines, or skipped procedures. Your friends may express condolences and support, but your heart will sink when you see how they respond to your lawyer's request that they testify in your favor. Insurance companies don't underwrite human loyalties.

The media will certainly report the accident and might even report the lawsuit when it is filed against you. However, unless the outcome of the lawsuit (two to three years later) is spectacular, it will be considered non-newsworthy. A settlement, or non-trial agreement, is even less likely to be reported. You are accused in the press, but you are seldom vindicated in public.

Moreover, regardless of the strength or weakness of your case, your insurance company may decide to settle simply because the cost of litigation is considered too high. As a result, even if you were not negligent, the plaintiff might walk away with a sizeable cash payment or annuity. You never had your day in court, but you still appear to be guilty in the eyes of your peers and most average Americans.

If you are sued, you will spend at least two years answering questions, reviewing documents, gathering information, reiterating explanations, finding witnesses, and reading and analyzing deposition testimony. In other words, you will likely work full time preparing your case. Liability insurance does not cover your lost earnings while you work with your attorney to prepare your defense.

Every pursuit in your normal working day will remind you of the tragic accident. Your "second career" as a defendant will force you to become intimately familiar with accident-related details, such as the brand of gear the victim wore or the weather or water conditions on the day the accident occurred. You will constantly replay "if only" scenarios in your head. If you are married, you can expect that relationship to be affected. Every day will be a bad day as you are haunted by this prolonged, seemingly obsessive need to revisit the past.

Even if a jury finds you innocent, you will probably be stigmatized in your community for the rest of your life. In fact, statistics show that most instructors and guides forced to defend charges of wrongful death or serious personal injury either leave their community or the profession. Frequently they leave both. No insurance policy or attorney can protect your professional reputation from such insult.

In summary, if you like what you're doing now, and want to continue your present lifestyle, there simply is no substitute for learning to minimize inherent risks and manage an incident. You may think you're already doing enough by working hard to prevent an accident from happening in the first place, but accident avoidance is only one aspect of effective risk management. If you want to protect yourself as well as your students, start by learning about what to do before a mishap occurs. And remember, the best insurance coverage in the world will not protect you from the horrors of being unprepared for that tragic emergency.

Negligence

The legal consequences of an outdoor accident depend, in large part, on the concept of negligence. To summarize the law of negligence, a provider (which in this case is the outdoor or adventure agency and its instructors, guides, or managers) has a legal duty to conform to a standard of care in order to protect its students or clients from an unreasonable risk of injury. The standard of care is generally higher for a provider who possesses, or presents itself as possessing, special skills (such as expertise in an outdoor activity) than it would be for an untrained, ordinary person. An outdoor or adventure agency must also meet a community standard of care, which is a level of skill and knowledge that is possessed by other similar members of the same occupation. Any violation of the standard of care that results in injury or death to a protected person such as a student or client can be considered negligent.

Negligence can be further defined by examining these four components: 1) a duty to act, 2) a breach of that duty, 3) harm, and 4) causation. A brief look at each can help you understand what it takes to be considered negligent.

If you are employed as a leader or guide, certain expectations will come with the job. Part of your duty demands that you act as someone else in your profession (who is in a similar position) would act when it comes to providing services to your students. It is accepted that outdoor leaders, for instance, are trained and prepared to carry out normal procedures of their activity according to an accepted industry standard. The duty might mean you must have at least a minimal level of training before going into the field. It might mean you will need to provide a certain level of supervision, carry emergency equipment, and know what to do in an emergency. If you are a volunteer who is working as a leader, you may be held to the same standard.

If you deviate from that standard, you will have breached your duty. If you perform in a manner that differs significantly from your equally trained peers, for instance, you will be acting outside the norm. If you do something that is generally not accepted within the industry (such as allowing your students to rappel on an old hemp rope you found), you will have breached your duty. It can also be considered a breach if you didn't do something (such as learning about the medical background of your students) that you were expected to do. If you are not sure what is accepted within your industry, you have a responsibility to find out. If you are ever in the position of wondering what would be expected, remember that your actions will be compared to what a reasonable and prudent person would have done in the same situation.

Just because you deviate from the industry standard does not mean you can expect a lawsuit. The final condition that must be present in negligence is that your actions (or inaction) resulted in, or in some way "caused" harm. If the student who rappelled on the hemp rope, for instance, fell to his death because the rope failed, your action (of letting him use the rope) was at least partly responsible for his death and you can be considered negligent. If, on the other hand, your student was thoroughly prepared to rappel, was wearing and using quality gear, was taught the proper steps and techniques (as understood in the industry), was using a newly purchased UIAA approved 12 mm rope, yet fell to his death anyway because the rope failed, it is highly unlikely your actions will be proven negligent. Although there was obvious harm, your actions did not cause the death in the situation described.

From a defense lawyer's perspective, effective risk management is achieved through a combination of learning, preparation, organization, and planning. You must understand the industry and industry standards, maintain your training, and be willing to act as a prudent and reasonable professional. But just as importantly, all these activities must be documented. Documentation helps the organization and instructors keep track of all the details, and it allows an attorney to defend them effectively after an accident.

Drafting Releases

Although some people believe that releases will not hold up in court, the truth is a well-written release that is presented appropriately can be and has been used as a powerful, legal document. In fact, a well-written release is typically an agency's first step toward establishing informed consent. Unfortunately, drafting such a document is not as easy as it first appears. As a matter of public policy, every agreement that frees a person or agency from blame is immediately suspect. Ambiguities in the document will usually be construed against the drafting party (or outdoor agency), which usually is the beneficiary of the release. Further, any plausible evidence that challenges either of the form's two distinguishable concepts (of "informed" or "consent") will severely hamper enforcement of the document. For these reasons, it is essential to have qualified legal counsel assist in the crafting of the release.

Releases are filled with esoteric clauses that the average person is unlikely to understand. Depending upon state and federal law, location, and circumstances, a release might also include a waiver, an acknowledgement of risk, an assumption of risk, a hold-harmless provision, and/or an indemnification agreement. Without the help of counsel, few adventure agencies are qualified to decide which elements are appropriate for the circumstances. As a result, few releases written by laymen contain the correct components or achieve the desired protections.

A common mistake is to take a form document such as another agency's release and modify it for your own purpose. State law requires a qualified description of inherent or other risks, and what's appropriate for one activity may not work for another. A releasing document drafted for whitewater rafting, for instance, might be inadequate for a mountain climbing or skiing course. You may do a fine job describing a series of potential risks associated with the activity, but without a trained lawyer you are likely to miss the legal implications of that word "inherent."

Releases have other nuances that are often missed or misunderstood as well. For example, the concept of "assumption of risk" has been interpreted and refined very differently by various state supreme courts. In some jurisdictions it has even been virtually defined out of existence. Further, the level of permissible assumed risk might differ from one activity to another. In at least one state, indemnification for attorney fees is not included among covered "damages" unless specifically listed, even if the paragraph describes "all claims, costs, fees, damages and other losses ...." These distinctions can inadvertently end up costing an agency untold frustration or monetary loss when they are overlooked by the uneducated author.

Releases should be easy to read, easy to understand, and free of archaic legalese and baroque writing styles. There is no place for "wherein," "hereinafter," "heretofore," "whereas," or "paragraph 2(b)(i)(A) below" in the document. Frankly, most modern lawyers spurned this jargon years ago. When these terms are used, it is often the result of non-lawyers, apparently believing that stilted argot somehow adds stature or enforceability to the form.

Instead, an effective release must convey legal concepts in plain, simple English. Short sentences should be used. A well-crafted release should be written for average Americans to understand quickly and easily; it should not be written for some legal luminary to unravel later. If a high school sophomore can't read and understand it, the release is potentially unenforceable.

A perfectly drafted release is worthless without the informed consent of the signer.

In summary, releases drafted by non-lawyers and hybrids edited by non-lawyers frequently contain fatal errors. After an accident occurs, the agency with the home-crafted release is often puzzled when the judge will not admit it into evidence or when the jury decides it is unenforceable. To avoid this unpleasant surprise, any outdoor or adventure agency that provides activities with inherent risks needs the active participation of qualified legal counsel in the crafting a quality and useable document.

Presenting Releases

A perfectly drafted release is worthless without the informed consent of the signer. A plaintiff's attorney usually defeats a release either by attacking the depth of knowledge the injured person had at the time of signing it or by challenging surrounding circumstances that tainted the participant's consent, implying that the release was signed with an element of duress. In other words, the context and the timing of consent are critical to later enforceability.

It's not enough to simply hand out the release agreements and ask for signatures. Every person who is expected to administer the release should be trained to know when and how to present it for signature. First, they must be clear about the level and depth of knowledge students are expected to obtain before they are considered "informed." Second, they need to be aware of how surrounding circumstances (such as perceived coercion) can affect the document's usefulness and enforceability. Lastly, they must learn to recognize and respond appropriately to comments made by the participants that warrant further analysis and possible remedial action (e.g., "Sure I'll sign it, but it's not worth the paper it's written on."). In brief, cautious, insightful presentation of a release is just as important as the quality of the document itself.

You may want to consider retaining your lawyer for an extra hour to write a script for the presentation of your release. Perhaps some photogenic person in your organization can narrate the agreement in a video presentation, clearly describing to your students the document they are being asked to sign. A short video such as this provides a vivid example of the information that was conveyed to the injured party prior to his taking responsibility for the risks, and it can later become powerful evidence to a judge and jury if necessary. If you choose to administer the release without the aid of an attorney, at least realize that there is an art to a well-timed and quality presentation.

Presentation of a release can be as important as the quality of the document itself.

Beginning students are, by definition, "uninformed." Therefore they cannot give "informed" consent before they know something about the risks that are inherent to the activity. Yet most companies make the mistake of presenting the release (along with other paperwork) on the first day of a course. Even worse, they might ask that the release be signed before the participants even arrive in town, and they fail to address the document at a later date.

Before students can agree to accept responsibility for a number of risks, an instructor must engage in some level of teaching about those risks. A dialogue should include a description and explanation of the hazards, and students should be given the opportunity to ask questions about them. Additionally, an organization might choose to redistribute the releasing document on one or more occasions after the course starts. Because students become more educated about risks as a course progresses, they can again acknowledge their acceptance by re-initialing and dating the form at the course's midway point. Repetitive review and reaffirmation also tend to overcome potential technical wrinkles that might have compromised an earlier consent.

The following routine provides a good example of how students can start to be educated about course hazards prior to addressing or signing the release. On the first evening of an introductory scuba diving class, the instructor passes out a summary of the most common risks inherent to the activity as well as a list of important policies or rules that will be used in the course. The rules, in actuality, are steps that will be taken to avoid or minimize the inherent risks. After this discussion, the students are asked to put their initials in the margin of the summary, near each policy, if they understand and are willing to abide by it. The instructor retains the initialed form and also leaves a copy with the students for their records. Then, and only then, does the instructor begin to discuss the release agreement that the students will be asked to sign.

Once the risks have been described and explained, participants are better able to give their informed consent. The presenter should emphasize the fact that the participant is being asked to assume responsibility for the risks and should take special care to ensure that the participants truly are making free and voluntary decisions, unencumbered by peer-pressure or deadlines. The presenter must expect and be prepared to answer questions as they arise. Most importantly, each presenter should foster an ambience of gracious and patient accommodation for anyone who hesitates even slightly in signing the release agreement. If a participant shows any sign of doubt or dissatisfaction, the provider should clearly tell her not to sign the document until and unless she fully agrees with it.

The presenter also needs to be particularly alert to remarks that might negate informed consent, and she should know how respond to such comments when they occur. Participants sometimes say things like "I'm signing this, but I sure don't agree with it," or "I'm signing this, but I know it's not enforceable." These comments cannot be ignored. The presenter should respond with a polite but firm assertion that the document was drafted by competent legal counsel and is indeed enforceable to the best of her knowledge. Other participants who overheard the exchange must also be reassured and forewarned that the document is enforceable. Any evidence of conditional or disgruntled consent should be considered a special circumstance that requires further discussion (and may even require an additional consultation with legal counsel) before the skeptic is allowed to participate in the activity.

Timing is another critical aspect when it comes to obtaining true and informed consent. Imagine, for example, the student who snaps "I wish I'd known more about these risks before I spent $649 on all this gear!" or "What? More paperwork when we're already here at the trailhead!" A participant is probably not making an unencumbered, free, and voluntary decision if she is handed a release agreement *after* she has committed significant time or money to the scheduled event. The same can be true if the student is handed a release at the eleventh hour, such as at the staging ar ea for a winter-survival weekend, on the bank of the whitewater river, or after the dive boat has left the dock. To avoid these challenges, releases should be distributed, explained, and signed in a relaxed environment *before* the participant makes any substantial personal or financial commitment, and *before* the participant has traveled to any location where a return to the point of origin is inconvenient, impractical, costly, or embarrassing.

The release-drafting and presentation steps described here require professional counsel and training. In order to learn from and avoid the mistakes that others have made, any agency that will be using or presenting a release should meet for a few hours with legal counsel to design the best presentation possible for all involved.

Medical Screening

Many outdoor and adventure agencies have adopted the practice of gathering medical information from participants prior to a course start. Unfortunately, they often act improperly once the information is obtained. The simple rule is, don't play doctor unless you are one.

Asking participants to complete a well-designed medical questionnaire at the beginning of or prior to a course is fine as long as the information is used appropriately. Too often, it is not. An instructor might be overly cautious upon noticing a participant's heart condition, for example, and be tempted to exclude that participant from the activity. Another instructor might allow a student into a course without recognizing a serious medical condition that could create problems. In both instances, the instructors were left to make decisions they were not qualified to make.

If you collect medical information from your participants, you need to understand the dos and don'ts associated with the process. A preferred, but admittedly expensive, option is to hire a physician to review all medical questionnaires before students are allowed to participate. If the physician has a question or concern about a medical condition, she could speak directly to the student about the situation or forward her concerns to the student's doctor.

Many organizations opt instead for using a physician sponsor. In this arrangement, a specially trained agency employee reviews medical questionnaires prior to a course start. When she identifies an unknown or suspect (contraindicated) medical condition, she notifies the physician sponsor. He, in turn, will talk to the student or the student's physician about the condition, voicing any concerns he might have.

If your organization does not employ a physician or have a physician sponsor, you might consider requiring a pre-course physical. If nothing else, when a student identifies a condition on his questionnaire that has not been addressed by a doctor, it is best to take him aside and privately tell him that you will need a doctor's written advice before he's allowed to participate in the activity. It will be in everyone's best interest to let the trained professional address whether or not the medical condition might in any way negatively affect his (or anyone else's) safety or well-being.

Whatever steps you use in your screening process, it is important for instructors to realize how the medical information is to be used once it is passed on to them. It is not to be used to make a personal call regarding participation. Instead, medical information can be used to help manage risk. For example, a student who suffers anaphylactic reactions to bee stings is not necessarily constrained to a life indoors. By obtaining information about the student's history and physical condition, an outdoor agency can inform the student about the likelihood of encountering bees in a given course area, and an instructor can make sure the student has epinephrine on hand and readily available in the event he is stung. This information will also aid in enabling the participant to make a truly informed decision regarding whether or not he is willing to attend the outing, knowing that bees will likely be present.

Further, by obtaining feedback from a licensed physician regarding the appropriateness of a student in your course, you will have added another level of insurance for your organization in the event something goes wrong. That is, you will have effectively placed yourself in the position of being able to say later, "I relied on the professional advice of a licensed physician." Without professional advice, you risk the sneering tones of a plaintiff's attorney cross-examining you with the leading question,

> *So, isn't it true, Mr. Quacksalver, that you reviewed the medical questionnaire of the decedent, and believed that your own wit and wisdom as an "accomplished ice climber" was far superior to a medical expert when deciding whether or not this lovely widow's asthmatic husband could scale that wall?*

Even if the cause of death seems to be unrelated to a medical condition, "relevance" is a soft, discretionary concept in law. Telling a jury to "ignore" a bit of evidence or an argumentative question is like telling someone to face the corner of the room and *not* think about the elephant that is standing in the middle of it.

The Americans with Disabilities Act (ADA) carries radical new implications for medical screening for outdoor and adventure agencies, and most of those implications have not yet risen to the level of public awareness. There was a time, for instance, when instructors and guides could declare a medical condition an "absolute contraindication" to an activity, without the further input of a physician. Today, no disabled person can be immediately, automatically, or summarily excluded from participation. All disabilities must be evaluated on a case-by-case basis, but few agencies have the medical qualifications to assess how (or if) the disability will affect the student's ability to participate. Years of practical experience are no substitute for an expert medical evaluation under the ADA. The only safe legal procedure is to employ a physician, use a physician sponsor, or send the person to a doctor for rejection or clearance.

If a participant identifies a disability on his questionnaire, and a physician provides a medical clearance, you will be expected to know and follow the rules as outlined by the ADA. The ADA requires that you decide (1) whether or not instructing this person poses a *direct threat* to the health or safety of others including yourself (but not including the disabled person); and (2) if that *direct threat* can be alleviated by *reasonable accommodations* that are *readily achievable* without a significant expenditure of money or time. If the student's participation does indeed involve a direct threat, he might not be appropriate for the course. On the other hand, if reasonable accommodations can be made with minimal effort, you will be expected to allow the student in the course and help him to succeed. This is a gross simplification of the legal standards and is intended simply to alert you to the general nature of the process. If you have any qualms or questions whatsoever, don't hesitate to seek the advice of an attorney.

Finally, the ADA means that the present standards of care in the outdoor/adventure industry must be reconsidered and possibly modified. In the past, an agency could simply say "no" to a disabled person who inquired about services, and a list of absolute contraindications was used to screen the disabled. As a result, the standards for field activities were designed with the assumption that all participants were fairly healthy and unimpaired. This practice is no longer acceptable.

In short, every adventure agency should be educated regarding the ADA and should have an understanding of what is meant by reasonable accommodations. The terms *direct threat* and *readily achievable accommodations* will have different meanings and applications in different activities. The point is that an organization is often, unfortunately, left to its own devices and exposure to litigation because newly evolving standards are unknown or unclear. Something must happen to precipitate a collective consciousness that will help guide individual organizations in the modification of standards for the positive purpose of teaching and working with disabled persons.

It will probably be many years before direction and assistance is offered in how to adjust the universal standard of care to accommodate the new measure of risk defined by the ADA. In the meantime, outdoor and adventure agencies will be left to their own discretion and good judgment in deciding how best to proceed.

Continuing Education

Knowledge knows no equilibrium. An outdoor instructor either learns continuously or forgets slowly. A guide who is content to rest on his laurels in the comfort of believing he has "arrived" at expertise is actually in a state of mental atrophy, destined to failure and to possible tragedy. When an instructor loses the curiosity to learn or the energy to hone skills, he is ethically obligated to retire from teaching in the outdoors.

Likewise, industry standards are constantly changing, embracing new technologies, challenging conventional wisdom, reacting to new laws and regulations, and accommodating shifts in user groups. No outdoor agency or instructor can avoid potential negligence without being currently knowledgeable about these ever-shifting standards.

Just as knowledge knows no equilibrium, skills are not static. They are always either improving or deteriorating. An instructor cannot manage risks in the field if he is not physically fit to engage in the sport robustly, vigorously, heartily. A sturdy, trim, obviously healthy guide with a history of regular exercise is far more credible to jurors than a flushed, flabby instructor breathing heavily from the walk to the witness stand—particularly if the testimony is, "I did everything humanly possible to hold him on the ledge." Regular (including off-season) exercise and ongoing practice of skills are essential elements of continuing education, which in turn is an essential element of risk management.

Have you changed what you teach or how you teach it in the past five years? Are you still using an outmoded or obsolete skill because you don't like the new technology? Do you take comfort in the simplistic justification that "we've always done it that way" or "it's always worked just fine that way in the past?" If you have held on to long-standing ways of doing things, your rationale may be correct. On the other hand, you might be hanging on to old techniques simply because you haven't kept up with the changing times.

When an instructor loses the curiosity to learn or the energy to hone skills, he is ethically obligated to retire from teaching in the outdoors.

Question conventions. Avoid dogmatic beliefs and mechanical routines. Allow for the possibility that your instructional practices can be improved. Skills and teaching methods must be adapted to new user groups (e.g., younger students or disabled participants) and new teaching methods. As a leader, you cannot afford to let your skills and methods sink into a rut of rote procedures.

Continuing education should include a healthy mixture of reading professional publications, participating in workshops, and attending conferences or symposia to see new technology, meet new people, and exchange ideas. A conscientious leader will also study accidents and near misses that have occurred within its program and elsewhere. Analyze the circumstances, join in dialogue, and write reflections about the events so that you can give definite form and structure to your thoughts. Incorporate these analyses into lesson plans and use them in a positive way.

Accidents can provide worthy learning opportunities, but it's also wise to be a little wary of the "facts," particularly in the immediate aftermath of an accident. Attorneys and institutions defensively suppress information during the statute of limitations period. Reporters and newscasters work on deadlines, which can interfere with their ability to be accurate and complete. If the principals aren't talking, the media may turn to third-party observers for speculation and "best guesses." Internet users officiously fill chat rooms and news groups with rumors that are often far from the truth. As a result, it can be tempting to develop judgments and conclusions when you should instead be looking for enlightenment. As Sherlock Holmes said, "It is a capital mistake to theorize before you have all the evidence." Be cautious with conclusions, but do not let the difficulty of obtaining evidence discourage you from engaging in accident analysis.

Attitude

Attitude plays an important role in risk management. If an instructor truly and sincerely wants to share his love of adventure with others, it follows logically and almost automatically that he will nurture and protect his students. However, if he is bored by the routine of leading novices and sees the next trip only as a paycheck, he may not have the same incentive to safeguard these new enthusiasts. In the latter case, risk management becomes work, an effort rather than a labor of love.

Passion can be one of an instructor's most valuable assets. Never take your passions for granted. Instead, nurture them, feed them, hone them like any other skill. An instructor who loves what he is doing takes measures to counter boredom and complacency and keep his passion alive. Continuing education is one method of doing this. Joining organizations and associations is another. Writing and publishing articles focuses your attention on what you know. Perhaps one of the best ways is to introduce a loved one, child, or spouse to an activity; their enthusiasm can be contagious. If you lose your passion, and nothing you try seems to bring it back, perhaps it is time to resign and find a new profession or job.

Attitude plays an important role in risk management.

Attitude can also have an effect on the legal actions taken after an accident or injury. An instructor who truly loves what he does and wants to share it with others will convey enthusiasm and confidence to his group. On the other hand, participants quickly sense when a leader has lost enthusiasm or is troubled, distracted, disorganized, unprepared, or unfamiliar with current gear or new methods. In the event of an accident, participants who see their guide as a respected mentor are more likely to take personal responsibility for any acts or omissions that contributed to the injury. Those who see the instructor merely as a commercial purveyor of knowledge and entertainment—and a bored or arrogant one at that—are more likely to seek litigation.

Risk management is more than an assemblage of perfunctory safeguards. It is a relational concept. If you treat a participant with genuine enthusiasm, concern, interest, and attentive care, that participant will probably respond in kind. Treat the student with little feeling, warmth, or interest, and those actions will likely be reciprocated as well. It is much easier to sue someone if you haven't caught their passion, felt their spark, or made a real human connection with them.

Know Your Students

Most instructors can think of a past student who had

"walking accident" written all over him or her. There are reasons why some people seem prone to accidents. Certain personality traits and behaviors are more likely to result in an accident or injury than others. Instructors must learn to recognize those behaviors and respond appropriately, either by advising the participant to change or by adjusting the field activity as necessary to protect the participant from his own maladaptive traits.

Start by asking participants why they chose to take part in the course. Watch for haughty machismo. Disabuse the thrill-seeker. Beware of rivalries. Separate dependent spouses. Do not tolerate chronic tardiness or habitual disorder. Don't ignore the obvious. Treat extreme awkwardness or clumsiness as a disability. Be wary of ulterior motives for participation (e.g., to save a marriage, start afresh from divorce, or to get in shape). Watch for reticence, indifference, and inattentiveness.

Highly trained professionals (such as doctors, lawyers, and Ph.D.s) may be older and more educated than their classmates, but as students of adventure activities they constitute a special high-risk category. They may come to the new experience burdened with the historical baggage of super-achievement, self-satisfaction, and too little time to stay in good physical condition. They usually have too much money, and they sometimes buy gear before they really learn what might be best for them. They may have read a lot and done a lot of other things, but for this activity their experience is no greater, nor their judgment any more refined, than other beginners. A concerned instructor should be alert for these traits and able to discuss them tactfully with the participant.

Students who enroll in advanced courses, on the other hand, have previous experience. But that experience can be a liability if it leads to bad habits or gives them a cocky, complacent attitude. What should be considered valuable knowledge and field time can ultimately become a disability that gets in the way of further learning. For instance, imagine an instructor explaining a point when a fixated student pipes in, "That hasn't been my experience." As the instructor describes a technique, the ace croons in again, "There's another way of doing that." For the good of the group as well as the safety of the individual, this person must be counseled before he becomes a hazard. It would be best to remind him that he can achieve the full benefit of the course by using his prior experience as a building block, not as a mental block.

An instructor is wise to document his students' personality traits—especially those that give cause for concern. The documentation should contain a written description of the behavior and any actions that have been taken to modify it. Writing crystallizes ideas and helps one see the nature and extent of problems more clearly. It can also help clarify the adequacy of remedial action. Written records illustrate the frame of mind of the instructor, the level of his concern for participants, and the level of his commitment to ensuring safe activities and exercises.

Documentation is also a powerful tool for the defense. A professional record, written before any accident occurs, is far more persuasive evidence for a jury than after-the-incident testimony that the decedent was an inveterate thrill-seeker, unwilling to heed caution. Criticizing the victim is always awkward and graceless. Jurors are uncomfortable with that kind of testimony and are far more likely to accept a prior written account because it was made while the thrill-seeker was still alive and with the intent of protecting him from future harm.

Organization and Planning

There is an old saying that goes "Failing to prepare is preparing to fail." For an instructor or guide, planning is fundamental to the process of building safeguards against inherent risks. In scuba, the aphorism is "Plan your dive, and dive your plan." If a plan is abandoned in the field, a significant element of preparation has been deserted as well. On the other hand, if contingencies have been properly anticipated, they will be incorporated into the plan and abandonment will not be necessary.

Good planning should occur well in advance of a scheduled event. As a part of this process, an instructor should review environmental factors, on his own as well as with participants. He should provide maps or sketches, supply equipment lists, and make sure that students are adequately prepared. An instructor is also responsible for making sure appropriate emergency equipment is available and in good working order (such as a first aid kit, repair kit, communication equipment, signaling devices, and other specialized items designed to deal with a field crisis).

Early in the preparation stages, identify which participants have some level of medical training, and be prepared to use their skills in the field if necessary. An agency should have a clear system for transporting participants and gear to the field, and these procedures should be discussed with the students.

Planning is fundamental to the process of building safeguards against inherent risks.

At some early point in time, it is also wise to develop a very detailed schedule of events. Make the itinerary realistic. Allow ample time for participants to accomplish the performance requirements in comfort, but do not leave large blocks of time unaccounted for. If necessary, consult a more experienced instructor or guide to discuss methods for improving your agenda.

Distribute and discuss the schedule with the participants. It will comfort them to know what will be happening and when. It will also give them confidence knowing that their leader is organized and prepared. On a subtler level, the detailed agenda will alert participants early on that time will be precious during the trip and that they share an obligation to keep the group on schedule.

As the outing gets closer, use a checklist to make sure nothing is forgotten, and inspect all equipment to be sure it is in good working condition. If you first discover defects on the eve of departure, it may be too late to make repairs and obtain replacements.

The day before your outing begins, check weather reports, water flow, and any forecasts that might be applicable to you and your group. Assemble last-minute items such as perishable food, drinks, and fuel. And notify or remind your employer of the schedule of events, your anticipated route, and your expected time and date of return.

At the staging area, re-evaluate environmental conditions. Engage in a pre-trip briefing with the participants. Review emergency procedures and identify the location of first aid kits, radios, and even car keys. Review the route, and reiterate the hazards that may be encountered. Obtain weather forecasts regularly and as long as possible into the event.

Leave nothing to unspoken presumption. This is no time

for poor communication, truncated phrases, or vague gestures. Speak loudly, clearly, and if necessary, from an outline in the field book. Check off each subject of your final briefing as you address it.

A contingency should be identified in case the weather degenerates or seas become stormy. A good plan should have made allowance for such changes. If there is a Plan B, don't be afraid to implement it. If there is no Plan B, don't be afraid to abort the trip. Do not pursue another route unplanned. Not only is it unsafe, but it also sets a poor example for participants. They are watching you and learning from your example. They have a right to expect a high standard of care.

The primary value of planning is that it leads to effective risk management. There is, however, a secondary benefit as well. The notes, schedules, checklists, and documents you create can form a valuable packet of contemporaneous records, revealing to a jury the meticulous preparation and planning of a conscientious provider along with a detailed account of precisely what happened every moment of the trip.

Measuring Achievement

Every adventure-based activity requires different fundamental knowledge or skills. If your organization is in the business of education, it is worthwhile to provide a means of measuring successful accomplishment of those skills in your students. This is especially true if the student expects to earn a certification of some sort or may move on to more-advanced training. It can also be important if a course is structured so that intermediate skills are taught (or intermediate challenges introduced) once entry-level skills are adequately performed.

Although success can be measured in a number of ways, depending on the activity, there is one common denominator for measuring *mastery* in all activities with inherent risks: Ask yourself, "Would I let my loved one [dive] [climb] [skydive] [raft] [kayak] with this person?" The answer is typically "no" when that person is a beginner. Initial or introductory training is typically little more than an entry-level license authorizing the novice to continue learning.

This observation about new entrants leads to three realizations. First, students must be taught that an elementary course of instruction will not make them accomplished performers. They should be encouraged to take more-advanced classes, practice their new skills with more-experienced friends, and be cautious about exceeding their training or comfort levels. These caveats should be written into lesson plans and emphasized repeatedly during the course of instruction.

Second, instructors must be cautious to never tax a newly trained student beyond entry-level challenges until he or she is ready. Beginners seldom have sophisticated critical judgment about the extent of their abilities. If the (respected and more accomplished) leader even suggests a higher level of challenge, the novice is likely to go along, assuming that the instructor "must think I'm capable of doing that."

Instructors should also be alert to the "toddler syndrome." Infants, taking their first steps, are usually cautious approaching a staircase. Adults, walking instinctively, approach a staircase with hardly a thought. Toddlers, however, are at an in-between stage. Having learned the skill already, they approach the staircase with unwarranted confidence, and occasionally, unfortunately, they tumble to the bottom. The toddler knows the skill but has no ingrained sense of foot placement. Newly trained participants in adventure activities face similar risks in the early stages of their development, and the apparent confidence of a new participant is often an inaccurate measure of his or her skills.

The third realization is that entry-level training is little more than a license to learn. In at least some adventure-based activities, there is a disproportionately high accident rate among new entrants. Clearly then, accurate skill evaluations are critically important if the beginner is to graduate to higher-level training.

This third conclusion can create a dilemma for an instructor, mainly because achievement and success include a number of variables, including judgment. And, as Simon Priest points out in Chapter Two, not only is judgment difficult to assess, it is almost impossible to develop until you have ample experience. The beginning student clearly needs more experience before attaining mastery, but it is likely unrealistic for the instructor to retain the novice until that level of mastery has been achieved. Consequently, it must be clear to students and instructors that the standard for successful completion for many introductory courses does not require mastery but only adequate "performance" of given skills.

To address this final issue, an agency or instructor should develop precise performance requirements for its courses (i.e., goals and objectives), and must then insist that no student "graduates" without satisfying the requirements for each (in the correct order of achievement if priorities are a part of the standard). Releasing a beginner into the field for unsupervised practice is already a dubious proposition. But if the novice has not met all performance requirements, it could be disastrous as well.

It can help if you prepare an evaluation form for each student, itemize every requirement (whether the goal is for performance or understanding), and carry the information into the field. Use an all-weather field notebook or waterproof bag. Photocopy erasable pages before cleaning to preserve information for the files. As soon as a student has demonstrated successful performance of a skill with the proper technique, the instructor should immediately record completion on the form. By making immediate entries, the instructor is recording the exact level of accomplishment of the student at every moment during the field training. As previously noted, contemporaneous records are far more valuable in court than unsupported oral testimony that recalls the event months or years later.

In summary, performance requirements in most entry-level courses do not indicate mastery of the activity. Rather, they presume that the novice has achieved little more than a license to learn. Mastery will come later, after the student has gained more experience and refined judgment, qualities that are beyond the scope of the beginner. Nevertheless, accurate and thorough evaluation at this level can be critical. Instructors must create and retain documentary evidence that clearly shows defined and prioritized performance requirements or course objectives. Evaluation forms should indicate that the student did indeed demonstrate each and every performance requirement before passing to the next level.

Gear Inspection and Maintenance

Most accidents are caused by human error, but many injuries are blamed on defective gear. Today's technology provides a high level of assurance that gear will function in good working condition if it is properly inspected, serviced, and stored. A well-documented history of this meticulous process (including purchase dates, maintenance history, and storage information) is the most effective way to prove later that the gear did actually function in good working condition.

An agency's equipment storage area should have a prominently displayed wall calendar with regular inspection and servicing dates recorded in bright colors. The area should have a tickler system in the front of inspection and servicing logbooks, and the logs should contain historical data (complete to current entries) describing the entire history of each piece of safety gear.

Every item of safety equipment should be readily identifiable by a serial number, a number written in indelible ink, or some other obvious feature. The servicing and repair logs should have separate pages dedicated to each identified piece of gear. This format allows easy, quick review of the history of inspections and repair for any particular item.

The equipment should also have an appropriate place in storage, and should always be stored in its place. Most items should be stored in a manner designed to avoid deterioration or damage from dampness, heat, direct sunlight, exhaust fumes, sharp edges, heavy blows, electromotive forces, and microwave emissions.

Gear should be cleaned and dried as soon as it is returned from the field. Returned items should be inspected for damage before being replaced in inventory, and the date and condition should be recorded in the inspection log. If an item requires repair, it should be stored temporarily in another location where it cannot be commingled with functional inventory. The defect should be recorded immediately in the maintenance log. When the gear is repaired, that repair should be described and dated as well.

Incident Management

In spite of your best efforts at planning, in spite of the careful attention you paid all along the way to managing risks and protecting your students from harm, the worst can still happen—you've just had an accident. What now?

Most outdoor instructors and guides have never witnessed a serious incident or death in the field. When it happens, it is very traumatic. An otherwise cool, skilled, and perceptive leader is likely to respond abnormally or impulsively. Defense attorneys see it repeatedly. A grieving person's ambivalence can be easily provoked into resentment, which quickly degenerates into litigation. Guileless comments and actions become damaging evidence and incorrect admissions. Media misinformation spreads irretrievably. Things can go quickly from bad to worse.

Case #1 Two hours after the death of a participant, the provider reported to the press that the fatality was caused by the decedent's own errors. When that statement was printed in quotes, the bereaving family immediately hired a lawyer who demanded a retraction, then proceeded to file a wrongful death lawsuit. Six months later, the autopsy clearly established that the outdoor agency was correct. Its mistake was saying too much too soon.

Case #2 A diver drowned alone, entangled in a fishing net. His body was immediately delivered to the pathologist for a routine autopsy to rule out foul play. In compliance with customary health practices, the staff of the coroner's office incinerated all of the decedent's apparel that was not claimed within 48 hours, including his latex dry suit. Later, in a wrongful death civil case, serious legal questions arose as to whether known prior defects in that dry suit had been properly repaired, or possibly had recurred that fateful day, leading first to panic and then to the fatal entanglement. Some other dive gear had been properly sequestered, but no one realized that coroners incinerate "clothing." Critical evidence was lost. The manufacturer's insurer paid a six-figure settlement.

Case #3 The death of a participant was initially attributed to equipment failure. Engineers employed by the manufacturer exchanged internal memoranda, in which they decided that a small internal part was probably too sharp on the edges. They immediately initiated a recall and replaced the part with a new design. The family of the decedent eventually sued the manufacturer for wrongful death. As the case unfolded, experts determined very convincingly that the death was not caused by gear failure. Nevertheless, defense counsel was strapped with these highly incriminating memoranda of impulsive employees, which made the very competent expert testimony appear self-serving and dubious. A very large settlement was paid.

Case #4 A well-meaning program manager rang the widow's doorbell two days after the death of her husband (the participant) and boorishly handed her a blood-stained bag of dirty gear along with a bouquet of flowers. He then exclaimed, "Boy, I never thought he'd do something like that." She was understandably furious. She broke into tears, began beating on the man, and screamed, "You killed him! You killed him! You killed my husband!" She threw the bag and the flowers down the stairs and slammed the door. A lawsuit was filed within a few days. It was settled with a seven-figure annuity two years later.

In each of these case studies, and many others like them, the problems could have been minimized or even eliminated if the people involved had been properly trained beforehand in how to manage the incident. Although it might be uncomfortable to prepare for an accident, all good risk management plans outline what should be done once the unthinkable occurs.

The Accident Response Plan

Every outdoor and adventure agency should have an accident response plan stored in a desk drawer, ready to implement at a moment's notice. Rest assured there will not be sufficient time to formulate one after the incident occurs.

As one risk manager has observed, "Without a plan, pulling people together after the incident is like trying to herd cats."

The plan should contain simple instructions to the staff on such matters as who to contact and how to organize and treat participants after an incident. It should also address rescue and recovery procedures, how to preserve gear and other evidence, and who to contact for assistance in completing incident report forms. Each organization should have a trained spokesperson, and staff members must be admonished that the appointed spokesperson is the *only* one authorized to speak for the agency. All inquiries and requests should be referred to him or her.

Every outdoor and adventure agency should have an accident response plan stored in a desk drawer, ready to implement at a moment's notice.

Long before an incident ever occurs, the organization should appoint a sincere, articulate employee to be that spokesperson, a role that should not be confused with the role of policymaker. The spokesperson must be familiar with the activities the agency conducts, and must be trained in communicating information with compassion, providing information while preserving defenses, and speaking about the incident in a manner that both recognizes the tragedy and reinforces the positive aspects of the activity.

It is also important to appoint or retain a lawyer as part of your incident response plan. As part of the planning process, before there's ever a need, the lawyer and the spokesperson should work through the details of how they plan to work together. Define the roles of this lawyer very carefully. Generally, practicing attorneys are not good spokespersons. They stand before the media like diplomats, fastidiously selecting words to describe the official view. They tend to be too cool, too analytical, too obviously cautious. They also tend toward reasoning at a time when family, friends, and the public are looking for compassion. As Tim White of the National Ski Area Association once said, "People don't care what you think until they know you care."

With the right spokesperson out front, your lawyer can be a valuable consultant behind the scenes. Under certain controlled conditions, your lawyer can become a conduit for sensitive inquiries and communiqués that will be treated later as legally "privileged" information, or an "attorney work product," not discoverable if the matter degenerates into litigation. Lawyers are trained to "peel the onion" in a manner that can provide insightful analysis for the spokesperson and for other policymakers after the incident. They can be artful wordsmiths in the positive sense of coaching the spokesperson to use the correct words and correct terms. Lawyers may also be doomsayers, but they are very sophisticated doomsayers. They speak from daily experience in a world most spokespersons and policymakers avoid.

Lawyers also tend to be a fairly domineering breed, and they may take control if you let them. Left unchecked, an attorney may quickly dominate the management of the incident, leaving the incident plan in ruin. However, if the lawyer is identified prior to an incident and brought into the development of the plan with a clear understanding of the roles of different people, this disruption is far less likely to occur.

Your own lawyer will need to be actively involved during the first days, weeks, even months after the incident, because insurance underwriters seldom retain defense counsel during this early period after the event. The unfortunate fallout from this economy is not only the loss of legal counseling for the potential defendant, but also the possible loss of valuable testimony and evidence.

Early interviews are important because the perceptions of witnesses change slightly every time the event is reported, and every time one witness speaks with another witness (who invariably has a slightly different perception of the event). Doubts diminish and convictions harden over time. Evidence sometimes disappears. While non-lawyers frequently conduct the actual accident investigation, the "work product" that they create usually enjoys special legal protections when performed under the auspices of retained legal counsel. Finally, even if insurance defense counsel enters the case promptly, it's still best to have your own attorney on the spot immediately, providing advice to you and your spokesperson as you implement your response plan.

Another ingredient in pre-planning for an incident is the preparation of an information packet or "talking paper" about your program and its activities. The media operate under deadlines. If a reporter does not understand an activity and is coming up on deadline, he or she is likely to consult the nearest available "source" and write what that person has to say about the activity—even if it is wrong. Misinformation that appears on the front page may at most be "corrected" with very few words in a one-inch column, on the inside, the next day. Misinformation on nightly TV news will probably never be retracted. Therefore, it is important to provide the media with a packet of thorough and reliable background material.

Information packets should be ready at all times, with multiple copies available for distribution to the media if and when necessary. Each packet should include a simple but detailed description of the particular activity or course, written for people who know little about it. It should give the media a clear explanation of the safety procedures that are used by instructors and participants to minimize inherent risks. It should also include statistics showing the history of safe participation, including references from other reliable and authoritative sources. To be effective, it cannot be merely a packet of propaganda printed on glossy paper with cheery bright colors and smiley faces. It must contain a plain, simple, straightforward, accurate, and highly credible general introduction to the activity.

Prepare a cover sheet for the packet, listing the names, addresses, and phone numbers of reporters, news anchors, newspaper offices, radio stations, and TV stations in your area. Very soon after an accident, someone in your agency (such as your spokesperson) should phone those numbers and notify reporters that this information packet is available.

If your agency is unprepared to respond to a crisis and provide such information, the news media, including the Internet, can become a potential hotbed of misinformation. Reporters who cannot get information directly from a credible source will find bystanders or other "experts" to fill in the gaps. Rumormongers gravitate to chat rooms, news groups, and bulletin boards, spreading gossip, hearsay, opinions, innuendo, and outright falsehoods: "I climbed that ledge three years ago, and I know the cousin of the paramedic who said he said that he saw …," or, "I believe this death was probably caused by the technique I've criticized publicly."

To minimize this exposure, the media information packets should also be posted on the Internet sites where rumors and misinformation are most likely to develop. After an incident, someone should be assigned the task of monitoring all news media (including these sites) and reporting misinformation to the spokesperson and others managing the incident. Whenever possible, the rumors should be corrected quickly. (Even eyewitnesses are influenced eventually by widespread conventional wisdom pertaining to "what really happened" on that fateful day.) But beware: If you are unfamiliar with the media or are unprepared to speak on behalf of your program or activity, you may find yourself facing greater frustration when your "corrections" turn into ongoing misrepresentations in the paper or on TV.

Summary

Traumatic death often comes quietly, in the calm of a seemingly routine event—no raging storms, screaming voices, and crashing noises. Everything is fine one moment and shockingly unreal the next. If everybody has been trained properly, all of the right people will be notified promptly, injured (as well as uninjured) participants will be managed sensitively, the rescue or recovery will unfold efficiently, and gear and evidence will be safeguarded. The agency can be confident that lawyers and a competent spokesperson will mobilize quickly and effectively. The press will be given useful information that helps them understand the activity, its inherent risks, and the safety precautions that were taken. Someone will interview witnesses and preserve their testimony. Someone else will monitor the media and the Internet to correct misinformation and quell rumors. By being prepared, you are effectively expecting the unexpected and leaving little or nothing to chance.

The risk management and incident management techniques described in this chapter measurably reduce the probability of litigation. Even if an injury or death does result in litigation, the likelihood of a successful defense will be greatly enhanced by this combination of thorough, well-documented risk management strategies by all involved. This scenario is truly the lawyer’s dream for the best possible defense to present to a jury of one’s peers.

The Problem with No Comment

(Editor's note: The following addendum comes from attorney Reb Gregg, legal counsel for the National Outdoor Leadership School and past president of the Houston Bar Association.)

A program that experiences a serious incident is faced with three immediate needs: 1) dealing with the injured party and/or family; 2) dealing with the media; and 3) understanding what happened and preventing it from happening again. In order to meet these needs completely, however, an agency must determine how deeply it will have to dig to address the latter, and it will have to decide whether or not to share this information in order to meet the first and second needs. This issue poses an important dilemma regarding which course of action an agency should take, and what response will best serve the interests of the program and reflect its values.

The many serious incidents—including four deaths—with which I have been involved as legal counsel have persuaded me to believe that in many situations a reasonable approach to dealing with media and potential adversaries is one of cooperation and openness. This approach can be shown to be sensible in terms of cost and ultimate damages paid, reputation, and the efficiency of continuing operations. The adversarial approach, on the other hand, is costly, aggravating, and distracting. Often it enlarges the potential damages, and rarely is it good for the program's image.

In most serious incidents the important facts are quickly known or can be reasonably determined. After an initial and limited fact-gathering mission, competent counsel on both sides generally are able to assess fault and damages. Inevitably there will be disagreements regarding some facts, and perhaps regarding applicable law. If the disagreements are significant, the opportunities for compromise shrink. But we should assume that both sides are reading the same law and have, or will discover, the same facts. If they approach the case truthfully, they will generally evaluate it in the same way.

The program (potential defendant) should, after an early assessment, commit to a more thorough investigation of the incident if there is any reason to believe that such an investigation will add to readily ascertainable facts and understandings, or if the credibility of an outside investigation is deemed important. The review can be conducted in such a way that it is protected from discovery or publication; but a good argument can be made for committing to make the results available to the media and the family, either in the form prepared by an independent investigating party (or team) or as a report from the program itself.

Direct negotiations, mediation, or arbitration create a much more productive atmosphere than the hunkered down, "catch me if you can" approach.

There are three distinct advantages to taking this cooperative and proactive approach. First, both the accident victims and the public receive a clear message that the program wants to know what happened and wants to prevent it from happening again. The investigation and sharing of information tell people that this is a quality program, committed to dealing fairly with its clients. Second, unnecessary costs, staff distraction, and enlarged damage payments are avoided. Third, the program can demonstrate that it has an acceptable plan for obtaining pertinent information, thereby making independent investigations by other interested parties unnecessary.

The strongest desire of the injured party or family is to make some sense of what happened. For the party who is best informed to withhold information and empathy in the face of these needs is cruel. It also aggravates a relationship that otherwise can produce a resolution that allows both sides to continue with their respective lives with some degree of satisfaction.

When the results are known and information is shared, there will be disagreements regarding fault and compensation necessary to make the affected persons whole. But direct negotiations, mediation, or arbitration create a much more productive atmosphere in which to operate than the hunkered down, "catch me if you can," "I'm going to make you work for every piece of information you obtain" approach, which too often has prevailed in traditional personal injury litigation. The frustration, disappointment, and anger generated by this latter tactic understandably, and typically, increase the monetary damages sought and paid.

The cooperative approach also has the advantage of reducing the burden on staff and allowing the organization to get back to business as quickly as possible. The distractions of preparing a lawsuit and dodging the media take much-needed energy away from the organization's fundamental operations. Document production is both time-consuming and expensive, and time lost being interviewed by lawyers and testifying at depositions and in court can never be replaced. Regular participants in outdoor activities are, still, a group that responds well to the cooperative approach. They are more likely to reciprocate with cooperation and fairness. Even the general public is becoming smarter about the benefits of resolving disputes without the protracted, expensive adversarial courtroom battle.

The cooperative approach may not be suitable for all circumstances, nor is it readily endorsed by most insurance companies. Obviously, it is important to get the cooperation and consent of the program's insurance company before volunteering information to the media or others. Nevertheless, it is my experience that serious dialogue or negotiation generally will produce an acceptable strategy that serves the interests—monetary and otherwise—of all parties. The approach can work, and it deserves careful consideration by an organization's staff, board of directors, and insurance carrier.

The Role of the Media in Accident Response

By Ty Hardt © 2000

Written from a reporter's perspective, Chapter Five offers strategies that outdoor and adventure programs can use to foster positive working relationships with the media. The author, one of the first reporters on the scene following a University of Alaska Anchorage accident that claimed the lives of two mountaineering students, uses two contrasting case studies to demonstrate the importance of preparation and an effective media response plan. Suggestions for conducting press conferences and interviews are also provided.

As a reporter, my personal involvement with the Ptarmigan Peak tragedy was as unexpected as the accident itself. If it wasn't for the exceptionally warm weather that Sunday evening, I might have decided to stay home. Instead, my wife and I set out for a quick hike up Flattop Mountain in the Chugach Mountains just east of Anchorage. At the final turn onto the trailhead I was stopped, like many others, and told by the Anchorage Police Department that the area was closed due to "some sort of accident." A quick call to the TV newsroom confirmed that a full-scale rescue involving both volunteer and military crews was underway. A producer also told me that I would most likely be one of the first reporters on the scene, as the information had only recently been picked up off the police scanner. After the call, all I knew was that the accident had happened on Ptarmigan Peak, it involved a mountaineering course from the University of Alaska Anchorage (UAA), and some people had been seriously injured.

I was familiar with Ptarmigan Peak, having climbed it myself from both the north and south sides, and could only imagine what had gone wrong. As I approached the parking lot and trailhead, the questions were already forming in my mind. What were the climbing conditions like? Was it unusually icy in the gully? How high were the teams when the accident occurred? What kind of protection (anchors) was the group using? Did their protection fail? How experienced were the instructors? How experienced were the students? Could I tell this story through the eyes of survivors? Did other media outlets know of the accident? Would my photographer be able to get to the scene before the competition?

Even with the popularity of Alaska's backcountry, few media outlets knew anything about the university's Alaska Wilderness Studies program before that fateful day in June of 1997. Even fewer had ever heard of Ptarmigan Peak. To most news gatherers, terms like *couloir* and *plunge-stepping* were from another language. But all that was about to change. By the time the first National Guard helicopters were in the air, local reporters were already converging at the trailhead, and the media was trying to get a quick education on the program, the mountain, and the fall. Networks were calling for information. Details were coming across the wire. Reporters were checking in with their assignment desks. Speculation was mounting about the cause of the accident and the casualties.

Because the accident site was so remote, an incident command center had been set up at the trailhead, a full four miles from where the accident occurred. Information from the on-scene crisis teams had to make its way to the command center before it was released to the media, and as a result, news bits were often slow and incomplete. Although there were multiple agencies and more than a hundred rescuers on scene, the Incident Commander seemed to be spending more time answering questions from the media than he did controlling volunteers. Although reporters could see helicopters ferrying climbers to local hospitals, we could not see for ourselves what was happening on the ground.

Once the names of some of the victims were released, family members were called for interviews. Local climbing guides were contacted for route information. Calls were placed to a Seattle outdoor organization, The Mountaineers, to investigate the favored methods of roped descent. After the most direct route to the accident scene was closed, at least one print reporter took an alternate route and hiked four miles to capture the first on-site pictures and eyewitness accounts.

The flow of information was challenging, to say the least. Much of what we heard was conflicting, and many of the sources were suspect. For example, several hikers in the area at the time of the accident were happy to contribute what they saw, but accounts differed from witness to witness. By-standers and third parties began to speculate on the fine points of the tragedy before the assigned media spokespeople could contribute reliable data. Reporters quickly discerned that on-site rescuers were passing information along to state park officials before distributing it through the Alaska State Trooper spokesperson. Consequently, information and evidence presented by a Chugach State Park ranger was considered by many reporters to be more reliable and timely than news released by the troopers. Though the two agencies were not releasing conflicting information, their efforts were uncoordinated and did not effectively answer the media's mounting questions.

By-standers and third parties began to speculate on the fine points of the tragedy before the assigned media spokes-people could contribute reliable data.

The university's spokesperson, unfamiliar with mountaineering and the inner-workings of the outdoor department, was also flooded with questions he could not thoroughly answer. What were the standard routes on the peak? What climbing techniques were the students using? How appropriate were those techniques given the students' skill level and the conditions on the mountain?

Although details of the fall (such as the exact techniques used during the descent) were unavailable that first night, what was clear was the severity of the accident. A group of 14 climbers had tumbled nearly 1,000 feet down a snow slope. We learned that at least two people had died and many others were injured. We also knew that snow anchors (pickets and flukes), which would typically be employed under similar circumstances, had apparently not been used.

Reporters like myself wanted to know how such an incident could have taken place within the formalized structure of a university course. Hard questions needed to be raised and confronted: If the climbers' method of descent was "acceptable," as originally reported by the university spokesperson, what went wrong and why did the fall occur? And why did the class choose not to use snow anchors or a traditional descent technique (such as those described in *Mountaineering: The Freedom Of The Hills*, the manual suggested in the course's own syllabus)? Mindful of legal liability concerns, the university system would wait months for a series of internal and independent reviews before offering an explanation. Their silence only made things worse, as far as the media were concerned.

In many ways, the Ptarmigan Peak accident was a worst -case scenario come true. The rescue occurred in a remote location on a Sunday evening. With 14 people requiring emergency airlifts and medical care, the principals at the scene had their hands full directing recovery efforts. It was a setting that would have severely tested any organization's media response plan, and UAA's was not up to the test. The university's official spokesperson was not prepared to field the specific questions surrounding the accident or outdoor department. However, even if reporters had contacted employees from the outdoor department (AWS), relationships between the AWS staff and local media had not been established. Both sides, not surprisingly, were hesitant to trust the other.

In the end, the Ptarmigan Peak tragedy did more than claim the lives of two students. It also forced the university's outdoor department to take a good, hard look at itself. This examination came while under fire from the media and from an increasingly restless public—a difficult, ugly predicament for any institution. My intent here is not simply to critique the University of Alaska Anchorage's response plan, but also to offer insight into what reporters are looking for so that organizations can be better prepared to face the media prior to and after an accident. With ongoing effort and planning, you can increase your chances of creating a successful relationship with the media before an incident happens to you.

Media Relationships

Reporters are always on the lookout for good stories: It's their job, and it's also their passion. You can use this simple fact to your advantage by establishing friendly relationships and open lines of communication between your organization and members of the media.

The first step in developing what could become a lasting alliance is simply to introduce your organization or yourself to the people who report the news. You might start with a news conference to announce an award an employee received following a well-publicized rescue or to announce new equipment that's been purchased thanks to a local fund-raising drive. Did your course have an unusually high success rate in the backcountry this year? Let others know it. Is your organization taking a stand on federal regulations that would limit backcountry access or approve backcountry development? Perhaps you sponsored a clean-up drive at a local trailhead, or maybe you maintain a unique website that promotes low-impact camping. These are just a few of the topics that local media might be interested in. You can use any of a wide variety of events to introduce yourself to the various news organizations in your community, the very people who will be calling you if you have an accident.

With ongoing effort and planning, you can increase your chances of creating a successful relationship with the media before an incident happens to you.

It might also be helpful to put yourself in a reporter's shoes for a moment and think about the way he (or she) works. What might he look for in a story? In the simplest of terms, the news media produce stories that interest them. Every story that makes it to print, television, or radio must first pass the "who cares" test. As a news director, editor, or producer, I always start with the same questions. Would I care about this story? Are there others who might? Do I care about the characters? Why or why not? Are there unique circumstances that readers or viewers would find interesting? Can my audience relate to what happened? Could it happen to them? Will my story force those who watch or read it to ask themselves how they would react?

Reporters have a lot in common with their readers or viewers or listeners. They live in the same neighborhoods, send their children to the same schools, deal with the same kinds of daily joys and sorrows as everyone else in the community. The circumstances that collide to make a compelling story can and do affect reporters as profoundly as they do their audiences. In a world that demands an increased news presence, such emotion and dedication make journalists valuable. A story that is important to the person who wrote it has a good chance of being meaningful to the person who's reading or watching it as well.

When it comes to researching and presenting the story, reporters still ask the basic questions: They want to know who, what, when, where, why, and how. But today's journalists also strive to make a story personal. What did the climber go through while trying to make her way out of that crevasse? What was her family going through back at home? What training had she gone through to prepare for the trip? Was she a naturally resilient youngster who easily overcame obstacles while growing up? Did she carry the proper gear? What better source than the climber to tell us what happened?

Reporters work in a demanding and highly competitive environment. With expanded local news budgets, they are encouraged to involve themselves with the story and to spend a great deal of time covering it. Microwave technology allows television crews to broadcast live from almost anywhere, and crews feel pressure (because of the competitive nature of the business) to camp out at someone's doorstep if that's what it takes. As a result, it is harder than ever for victims' families, program managers, or even witnesses to be shielded from the camera lens, the microphone, the note pad. Today's information gathering and dissemination techniques weren't even developed, much less utilized, only a decade ago. But today's audiences expect and revel in this kind of instantaneous and extended coverage.

The tools may be changing, but the simple rules of newsgathering and writing have remained amazingly consistent. Reporters are still accountable to the ultimate authority of accuracy, fairness, and public demand. There is a great deal of responsibility associated with bringing the reader or viewer a story, and that responsibility is seldom taken lightly. Nevertheless, reporters do make mistakes. Depending on the staffing levels of the newsroom, filling two minutes of a newscast can cost the reporter days of tedious research and investigation. As a result, though reporters generally work hard, they sometimes steer for the easy road. If you are prepared, and if you have good working relationships, you can help the media, as well as your organization, by providing them with the information you want to convey.

The Media Response Plan

No matter how congenial your relationship with the media, it is imperative for your organization to have a media response plan in place, up to date, and readily available. The plan should be clear and concise, and all your employees should be familiar with it. In fact, an orientation into your organization isn't complete until every employee knows what to expect and what to do when it comes to dealing with news-gathering organizations. Just as you might require workers to have crisis-response training (such as first aid or search and rescue) for field emergencies, consider requiring similar crisis-response training for dealing with the media after an accident.

Just as you might require workers to have crisis-response training for field emergencies, consider requiring similar crisis-response training for dealing with the media after an accident.

The following list identifies some of the steps you and your organization should address when creating your plan.

- First, take the lead from other companies and organizations and assign one or two staff members to be personally responsible for media relations. This media contact person should be an excellent, compassionate communicator who should be responsible for authoring press releases and conducting press conferences. He or she should also arrange and be present at all scheduled interviews, and staff members should be instructed to refer media inquiries to him or her.

- Your spokesperson should have easy access to written background statements that can help answer reporters' general questions. These detailed statements might include your organization's mission, history, enrollment figures, hiring and training policies, and safety record. The plan might also contain up-to-date accident data drawn from national statistics. More information about this type of "working paper" is included in Chapter Four.

- It would be unrealistic for a single spokesperson to be intimately familiar with all aspects of a large organization, especially if the company does more than provide outdoor education services. Consequently, whether you choose to use a working paper (as described above) or not, if your agency is multi-layered, you'll need to have a system in place to make sure information is passed effectively from units within the organization to the agency spokesperson. In the event of an accident, you might want the spokesperson to meet with a unit representative before meeting with the media, for instance. At minimum, make sure comprehensive, up-to-date information (about each unit) is available for the spokesperson to review before he conducts a press conference or interview.

- In addition to background material, reporters covering an accident will want answers to the "The Journalists' Five W's:" Who are the victims, the rescuers, and the instructors? What exactly happened? When did it happen? Where did it happen? And why did it happen? Your media response plan should instruct your spokesperson to anticipate this type of questioning and be forthright, honest, and accurate about descriptive facts, subject only to legal restraints.

- In recognition of those restraints, your plan should also clearly outline legal and institutional restrictions governing the release of certain information. Your spokesperson should refrain from finding fault, assessing blame, or criticizing the conduct, policies, or equipment of any party until the incident has been fully investigated. Likewise, he or she should not discuss the specific nature of injuries or illnesses prior to their diagnosis by a licensed physician. Names of victims should not be released until their next-of-kin have been notified. In cases when information must be kept confidential, explain why. It is also a good idea to get legal advice and have these explanations written out in advance.

- It also pays to cultivate a working relationship with your local police, sheriff's department and/or state troopers. Learn the details of each of their media response plans. You may discover that they intend to release the very information you want temporarily withheld (such as the names of victims). If another agency's media response plan conflicts with yours, take the time to work out a compromise before your plan is called into action.

- Make sure your plan includes up-to-date and accurate phone numbers, fax numbers, and e-mail addresses for all local radio and television stations, as well as newspapers and magazines. Reporters *want* you as a source and their numbers are by no means secret.

- It may seem silly, but performing mock interviews in preparation for the real thing does make sense. Just as news anchors pre-read their scripts, you or your spokesperson can benefit from sitting down in front of a simple camcorder and practicing what you would like to say. Practice can ease your jitters before they even start. You may also want to make regular practice runs a part of your plan.

- Develop a system that allows your organization to archive old press clippings, or television and radio stories. This could include a simple scrapbook or a dedicated VCR and a box of tapes. It's a method that will instantly show you the differences between how various media outlets tend to approach the same story.

- Know the message you want to convey when you hold a press conference or write a release, and take care to ensure that all information is accurately conveyed and received. Remember that reporters are as human as you are. They will sometimes take the easy way into and out of a story by lifting important data directly from your press release. If it's wrong there, it will most likely be wrong in print or on the air. Likewise, it is a good idea to immediately confirm in writing any facts offered orally in an interview or press conference. Reporters welcome this: They too are concerned with accuracy.

- Once your plan is on paper, discuss its importance with

your staff and volunteers. Make it a part of your employee handbook, or at least review it with employees during orientations or staff meetings. The better prepared your entire staff is, the greater the chance your organization will respond effectively in the event of an accident.

Interviews can be unnerving and unsettling in the best of times; after an accident they can be a nightmare.

Smile for the Camera

In the aftermath of an unfortunate incident or tragic event, your response plan will be put to its ultimate test. Even the best-laid plan cannot guarantee affable interactions with the media at such a time. At some point, you (or your spokesperson) will be asked to hold an interview or a press conference. Interviews can be unnerving and unsettling in the best of times; after an accident they can be a nightmare. If you have any difficulty at all speaking in front of a large group of people, imagine that feeling magnified and captured forever by an impersonal camera lens. The good news is, it doesn't have to be that way. You will be more comfortable if you understand the process and know what to expect. Preparation can help you achieve the optimal outcome.

As the subject of the interview, you should have a firm grasp of exactly what information, ideas, or thoughts you are trying to convey. You must also be sure to convey them in the way you intend. If referring to notes would help keep you focused and on track, bring them along. Relate the information conversationally, as if you were sharing news with a neighbor. Interviews often sound canned and overly rehearsed. Allow yourself to sound human as you relay your main points.

Be prepared to bring reporters up to speed on the basics as well as the latest developments. Facts or scenarios that seem fundamental to you might be complex to the normal viewing audience. Do you know the difference between a fluke and a picket? The general public probably hasn't heard of either. Yet when a story involves a mountain rescue or accident, that information could be vital. On the other hand, don't assume the reporter is a complete novice. Many reporters are skilled at feigning ignorance and encouraging an interviewee to open up and offer potentially useful details.

If a reporter is doing a feature story, the interview will

probably be one-on-one. But following a major accident, interviews are more likely to be conducted by a group of reporters, all of whom will ask you questions. You may be asked to wear three or four separate wireless microphones. After the interview, you could also be asked to continue the conversation while cover video (also known as "two-shots") is being taped. If the interview is conducted in your office, crews might ask you to casually work from your desk for additional coverage. These sequences will be used later in the editing bay to make a smooth transition between the reporter's thought and the first line of your interview.

Although public speaking is still high on many people's most-feared lists, it doesn't have to paralyze or even worry you. Before you start down the path of dreading the experience, simply relax. Take a couple of deep breaths. Ask the reporter what will be covered and what questions to expect. Gather your thoughts. If the interview isn't being broadcast live, you can stop at any point if you need to. I'm often asked to begin again because the person I am interviewing forgot the point he or she wanted to get across. If you get tongue-tied or if you believe you've unintentionally misrepresented your organization, just start over. Reporters and photographers are used to it and will move right past it in the edit bay.

Expect to have the same question asked in a variety of ways. Be conversational and try to forget that the camera or microphone is there. As a matter of fact, looking into the camera during a taped interview is a bad idea, and the crew will most likely ask you to look at the reporter. The idea is for the camera to "eavesdrop" on a conversation, and that perception is lost when you look into the lens. Instead, keep your eyes on the reporter as you would during a normal conversation, and you won't have a problem. If you've never been interviewed, you may feel uneasy. The more you sit in front of the camera, the friendlier it becomes.

Reporters may get to ask all the questions, but you have motivations for the interview as well. You can use the opportunity to impart factual information that describes your side of the story. And don't be afraid to influence the process in order to create the story you want to tell.

Here's where preparation really pays off. Before the

interview begins, ask yourself what impression you would like to make. What points will it take to leave that image? Don't be afraid to use an outline. That way, if nerves get the better of you, you'll still have a point of reference. Also, your message is more likely to be absorbed if it is organized, brief, and well thought out.

If it appears that human error may have contributed to an accident, it is likely that legal concerns will shape your responses. You should be careful, for instance, to avoid the inadvertent comment that could place blame or the premature release of confidential information. Nonetheless, you can still use the interview as your opportunity to describe your program and mission, your accident record, and any other information that might help educate the audience.

If you are unable to answer certain questions, or if you simply don't know the answer, there's nothing wrong with saying so. In fact, "I don't know" is a much more appropriate response than the callous "no comment" or an uneducated guess. There can be a big difference between an accident happening at 10:30 a.m. and 10:30 p.m., for instance, or a victim being 18 rather than 28 years old. If you are unclear about an answer, tell the reporter you'll need to check on it and then do so. Those facts make the story, and their accuracy confirms your credibility as a source.

You should also be aware that anything you say could wind up on the air or in a story unless you have made it perfectly clear that the information is "off the record," and therefore off limits. Even after the camera stops rolling, remember who you're talking to. Just because the microphone has been put away doesn't mean the interview is over.

The questions raised following an accident aren't always directed only at the people associated with the event. Some times they're aimed at the media itself. Many wonder about the rights of victims, witnesses, and even course instructors. Shouldn't they be left alone? Don't they have the right to avoid the journalistic spotlight?

It is the media's point of view that when you become involved in a "spot" news event—intentionally or unintentionally—you forfeit your right to privacy. News organizations will cover any story deemed interesting or important to the public at large, and a backcountry accident clearly falls within these criteria. The press has the right to publish pictures from the scene and to quote witnesses. They also have the right to investigate the cause of the event, and it's quite likely they will try to hold someone accountable. This attention, however, has its own stringent statute of limitations; those in the spotlight today aren't necessarily condemned to stay there. As the newsworthiness slowly wears off, so does the obligation. The focus does fade eventually.

News organizations will cover any story deemed interesting or important to the public at large, and a backcountry accident clearly falls within these criteria.

The Importance of Being Prepared

In the event of a major accident, the media will be representing the public in its search for answers. Only your spokesperson will be representing you. As the old saying goes, you (or your spokesperson) will never get a second chance to make a first impression. This is why a respectful and congenial relationship with the media is so important. In that critical opening hour, when you first meet the people who report the news, you have the opportunity to set the tone for all future reports and interviews.

The first person the media will usually contact is your appointed media representative, and that person should be prepared to handle what could eventually become a waterfall of media requests. He or she should be a reliable member of your organization and thoroughly briefed on what to expect. In the interest of getting an accurate story out and protecting your organization from charges of indifference or stonewalling, this liaison should be willing to share his or her home phone number, pager number, or fax number with reporters and should also be prepared for an impolite 3:00 a.m. call as a reporter approaches deadline.

In order to illustrate the importance of that first encounter, let's return to the Ptarmigan Peak accident and compare the university's response with another Alaskan outdoor education program that had to answer comparable questions from reporters after an accident that occurred in 1999. The two situations had some similarities: students on a wilderness trip, a slip, and a disastrous fall.

Following the Ptarmigan Peak accident, the University of Alaska Anchorage (UAA) spokesperson was unable to answer many of the questions that were asked simply because he wasn't fully prepared. Although he was trained to handle the media, he was not able to provide details of the fall. This specific situation was further complicated because of UAA's multi-layered system. The spokesperson fielded reporters' inquiries after the accident, but he knew very little about the specifics of the outdoor department. Employees of the department were more knowledgeable, better prepared, and more willing to answer specific questions about the incident and program. Yet department representatives were ignored by the media as well as by a university strategy that failed to include them in its media response plan.

Two years later, the Alaska branch of the National Outdoor Leadership School (NOLS) found itself in a similar position, facing Anchorage's local media following an incident on the Matanuska Glacier (80 miles outside of Anchorage). A student was missing and presumed dead, and the media went looking for answers. NOLS's ability to answer reporters' questions was very different from UAA's, however, and their spokesperson, appearing knowledgeable and prepared, set an immediate tone of cooperation with local and national media.

Reporters first caught wind of the massive search effort a day after it had begun. A New Hampshire teenager disappeared from the glacier's surface Sunday evening while collecting water for his fellow students. By the time the National Guard rescue team landed on the ice, the local NOLS branch director had begun opening lines of communication with media representatives.

While film and rescue crews gathered at the scene, the NOLS director fielded questions from several reporting teams, including one driving a satellite truck to the edge of the glacier. The media quickly learned that 11 students, descending the glacier following a climb of Mount Marcus Baker, were several miles ahead of their instructors. One night at camp, the victim went off on his own to collect water, apparently slipped into a moulin (a hole in the glacier), and vanished.

Inevitably, reporters wanted to know why the students weren't supervised. Why was a 17-year-old allowed to travel on the glacier unroped? Many of the questions and concerns were the same as those surrounding the Ptarmigan Peak incident: Had NOLS been through a similar accident in the past? Who was the student? What was his personal level of climbing experience? The NOLS spokesperson was able to appease the media by answering many of the questions that the UAA spokesperson could not. He was able to provide background information about the program's mission and accident history in general, and the mountaineering course and route specifically. He explained that the students were in a "safe" area the night the incident occurred and therefore didn't need to be roped. And he was able to defend the practice of allowing students to guide themselves out of an expedition by saying, "It allows the students to really test their leadership skills." The media was told that an investigation would be conducted in order to learn more about the accident, and the spokesperson reported that additional information would be provided as it became available.

Even though the 17-year-old's body has not been located—a rock cairn has been left on the ice as a silent memorial—the honest conviction has paid off. An external review into the accident, which was promptly released to local news sources, recommended very little change to the program. Local and East Coast media seemed satisfied with the findings. Even the student's mother visited Alaska and donated money to purchase additional fiber-optic equipment in the event a comparable accident happens in the future.

The treatment given to the University of Alaska Anchorage and its outdoor program by the local media and public was far less supportive. While the university's administrators expressed deep shock and sympathy for the victims' families, their reaction did not temper the community's disbelief that such an accident could have happened. The university spokesperson, unfamiliar with the inner workings of the outdoor department, was unable to provide many details about the program, its mission, its accident history, the class, or the route. Acting on what some consider poor advice from legal counsel, the university maintained a reticence regarding the accident itself, which was interpreted by the media and public alike as a combination of ineptitude and cold obstructionism.

As the university attempted to dodge the media spotlight, interest in the story only grew stronger. Eventually, the university's lack of information and cooperation became the story. The outdoor program's director eventually went public over her frustration at being silenced. In the end, the university weathered a public relations disaster, painful internal disputes, and costly litigation.

As the university attempted to dodge the media spotlight, interest in the story only grew stronger.

What can other outdoor programs learn from the way UAA and NOLS handled their media response plans? Admittedly there were differences between the two accidents and it would not be fair to make an unconditional comparison. Nonetheless, NOLS's ability to provide information quickly and as openly as possible set the stage for a positive relationship with the media. In the university's case, however, the lack of information created an atmosphere of suspicion and animosity.

Using this comparison, it's simple to see the advantage of having open lines of communication and a trusting relationship between an organization and members of the local media. Further, the importance of a well-informed and prepared spokesperson cannot be understated. Public outcry and concerns surrounding impending litigation can admittedly complicate an agency's ability to speak freely. But a mishap, even a fatal fall, will not pique the media's or public's interest like an accident with an ensuing or perceived cover-up can. These issues, and all associated "what if" questions, should be anticipated and addressed in your media response plan prior to an accident.

Conclusion

The media is not the cannibalizing hyena it is sometimes made out to be. The packaging may have changed, but the content of a newscast, newspaper article, or radio report still depends on the basic five W's that have been standard journalistic concerns as long as reporters have been telling stories. A basic understanding of what reporters and editors require from a story can help you deal more easily with the media, and can even help you shape the way your story is covered and presented.

We all make mistakes, but it's how we handle these mistakes that makes or breaks the relationships between the media and the organizations we cover. The media made its own mistakes in covering the Ptarmigan Peak tragedy. Facts were unintentionally misrepresented—the height of Ptarmigan Peak, its relationship to Anchorage, the number of injured climbers—and even the wrong mountain peak was placed behind a reporter during a live shot. When that happens, it's up to that reporter to make it right. As an organization, you have the right to question the media with the same critical eye the journalist uses to examine you. Only when mutual trust and respect is established will the benefits begin to emerge.

When UAA's newly renamed Alaska Outdoor & Experiential Education (AOEE) program lifted the suspension on its mountaineering courses and fielded its first mountaineering outing two years after the Ptarmigan Peak accident, I was again involved as a reporter. This time, my story focused on the program's new equipment, revised safety standards, and the revival of a much-changed educational program. Ironically, the university and the media had finally developed a working relationship after two years of discord and distrust. In my case, that only happened after I was invited to review early drafts of AOEE's *Plan of Action* and then witnessed that plan put into motion. The department had obviously learned from the tragedy and was making detailed and conscientious steps to prevent another. Being offered fair progress reports on the university's plan helped reinforce its relationship with the media. And, not surprisingly, as the university further refined its connection with the media, its treatment by the media also improved.

Your community's media outlets play a crucial role in disseminating information and shaping public opinion. Though prone to human errors, journalists take this responsibility seriously and delve into their assignments with passion and professionalism. Knowing this, you should begin to foster a symbiotic relationship with the media. Be helpful, honest, and clear when providing reporters with information. Develop positive, personal ties before an accident occurs; don't allow your program to make its news debut with coverage of a tragic event.

Finally, don't underestimate the importance of a workable media response plan. Instead, think of it as one more item in your personal survival equipment. Because no outdoor education agency can predict when its next disaster will strike, the time to prepare is now. That dedication to your organization's future could pay off well before the plan is ever put into motion.

Ethical Foundations of Wilderness Risk Management

By Jasper S. Hunt, Jr. © 2000

This chapter addresses fundamental issues in the ethics of risk management in wilderness-based experiential education. The author examines the ethics of exposing people to risks and makes the case that ethical acceptability depends upon the organization's mission and the participants' informed consent. The chapter is based on a paper called "Ethically Acceptable Accidents in Wilderness Education," originally presented at the 1998 Wilderness Risk Management Conference in Black Mountain, North Carolina. The paper was later revised and presented at the 1999 International Camp Nurses Association Conference in Bemidji, Minnesota, and has been further revised for presentation here. Responding to concerns voiced at the first presentation, Dr. Hunt has disguised the names of the organizations from whose printed material and marketing brochures he quotes.

My first response when asked to write about ethically acceptable accidents was puzzlement. Isn't the very idea oxymoronic? How can an accident ever be justified? Aren't accidents, by definition, unethical and unacceptable? I also doubted my competence to tackle this issue. Surely, there must be someone more knowledgeable about accidents who should be writing this paper. Then I started thinking back over my career so far as an experiential educator.

It has been 30 years now since Jed Williamson gave me my first job as a sherpa at the North Carolina Outward Bound School, and in that time I've become familiar with a lot of accidents. There was Henry McHenry's fall in 1972; Don

Haldiman's fall in the Linville Gorge; the young woman raped while on solo at North Carolina Outward Bound School in 1971; Brad Shaver's death in the Himalayas; the two young women at Northwest Outward Bound School who died on final expedition in the Oregon Cascades in 1971; the University of Puget Sound students who died in an avalanche on Mt. St. Helens, while I was camped that very night about 1,000 feet below; Devi Unsoeld on Nanda Devi; Willi Unsoeld on Mt. Rainier; my own 30-foot leader fall in Boulder Canyon in 1982 that should have put me into a wheel chair for life; the 1989 NOLS accident on Mt. Warren where a young student died; the 1996 Everest expedition that has been so thoroughly written about and discussed; the 1997 University of Alaska Anchorage accident that killed two students and seriously injured many others; Craig Dobkin's fall several years ago that put him in a wheel chair. There are others. In running down the list, I realized that I have had a lot of personal experience with accidents, some of them with direct involvement and others from reliable second-hand knowledge.

I want to draw from my own experience as I approach this subject, but I am faced with a dilemma, one that is pregnant with meaning for me personally and for our profession in general. How do I use the accidents I know about as a source of moral education when many of the people who were directly involved or affected by them are still alive? An ethical analysis invariably leads to moral judgment. How dare I make a moral judgment about Willi Unsoeld, for example, or any other of the other people I know about and the situations they encountered?

One wants to learn from past experiences. But at the same time one must be very cautious about the effect ethical analysis may have on the memories of the dead and the sensibilities and welfare of the living. The goal here is to do ethical analysis, not to make judgments, to understand rather than to criticize or defend. Although ethical judgments will and must be made as well, they are for the most part beyond the scope of this chapter.

The Unacceptable Accident

Before we examine ethically acceptable accidents, it is

worth considering what makes an accident ethically unacceptable. And certainly one of those things is silence. The accident that is not openly discussed, not learned from, not held out as a case study for other practitioners and peers to examine, is an accident that is in its very nature unacceptable.

Several years ago I spoke with a Vietnam veteran about his experiences as a young 2nd Lieutenant of infantry in combat in the Mekong Delta in 1968. The issue of casualties came up. I asked him how he handled it as a leader when someone would get killed or wounded. Thinking along the lines of EMT training, I wanted to know how he would handle critical incident stress debriefs while in the field. It seemed reasonable to me that even in combat, a leader would conduct such debriefings after a wounding or death, once they were in a secure area and the action was over.

The accident that is not openly discussed, not learned from, is an accident that is in its very nature unacceptable.

The guy looked at me like I was crazy. He informed me that the helicopter would land, the body would be thrown on board, the chopper would leave, and the men would continue on with the mission. There would be nothing said about the death or casualty, ever. Years later it would become apparent that this silence may be one of the chief reasons so many Vietnam veterans suffered from post traumatic stress disorder. Failure of the leaders to offer any sort of debriefing to survivors resulted in psychological harm being done.[1]

I think it is legitimate to analogize from the Vietnam experience to an accident in an outdoor adventure program. A death or an injury suffered on an outing is often treated as a dirty little secret that we dare not talk about. We especially don't want to discuss the ethics of it all. It is interesting to note that once an accident occurs, one of the first things people are told is to not talk about it. The advice usually comes from legal counsel concerned about potential lawsuits. But that advice, sound though it may be from a legal standpoint, can interfere with both the healing and learning processes.

An accident not talked about or learned from is ethically

[1] *Interested readers can learn more about this topic from Jonathan Shay's* Achilles in Vietnam, *which provides an in-depth analysis of the consequences of failing to take seriously the impact of death and injury on soldiers. Col. Bob Rheault of Hurricane Island Outward Bound School has also played a leadership role in this area.*

unacceptable. Note that this is an after-the-fact argument. The aftermath of an accident can make it unacceptable, even if the accident itself is found to be ethically acceptable. Continuing with the Vietnam analogy, Dr. Shay argues that small unit leaders in the military have a moral duty to look after the psychological welfare of their soldiers. I argue here that we as outdoor educators have a similar duty to look openly and honestly at our accidents and share them with our professional peers.

This ethical duty extends outward in three directions. First, and most important, is the impact the accident has on the victim and his or her family and friends. Second is the impact of the accident on the students, staff, and administrators of the program involved. Third is the impact of the accident upon the profession of wilderness education in general. A proper response to any given accident can be very helpful to all three areas.

Another issue that may indicate an ethically unacceptable accident is boredom. Very often wilderness educators operate in areas where they have become very familiar with the terrain and its geographical and geological features. After someone has led student groups up the north ridge of the Middle Sister Mountain five or six times or more, it can become rather tedious to take another group up the same route. The same occurs with rivers, lakes, deserts, and other venues. I have seen many instances through the years where instructors have elected to take students on riskier outings, not because of a solid educational goal, but because the instructor is bored with the other, more predictable route. The students are placed in a riskier situation because of instructor boredom.

Why is this unethical? Let me again analogize. Imagine for a moment that you are an airline pilot. You have made hundreds—no, thousands—of takeoffs and landings at the same airport. You're bored, and you decide you need a little novelty in your professional life. So you order your co-pilot to shut off one of the four engines and land the plane using just the other three. It seems obvious that if a commercial airline pilot did this, he or she would immediately be out of a job. And there would be a good reason: The riskier landing added absolutely no benefit to the passengers and only served the needs of the pilot.

Boredom, however, is not the only reason an instructor might unnecessarily increase the risk for students; social status can also play a role. Staff members who take students on riskier routes are sometimes awarded higher status on the organization's social pecking order than instructors who stick to less risky routes. In the mountaineering and paddling worlds, for instance, social status is often directly correlated with the levels of risk an individual has encountered in his or her personal outdoor activities. The ethical danger emerges when they carry this measurement of social status, which may be appropriate for one world, into their work with students under their care.

I will never forget hearing the late Paul Petzoldt, legendary mountaineer and wilderness educator, say that just because an individual has pioneered a new route on Mt. Everest doesn't mean he or she is automatically qualified to teach students. The character traits needed to achieve mountaineering greatness may be very different from the character traits needed to achieve excellence as a mountaineering instructor. Indeed, there may even be, on empirical grounds, a negative correlation between the extremes of risk presented on a climbing or paddling resume and the qualifications necessary for outdoor leaders. The willingness to continue doing less risky routes may be a significant virtue for an outdoor instructor, rather than a negative character trait. Program administrators need to be alert to this issue of social status and diligent in assessing its effects within their organizations.

Telos and Risk

Classical Greek philosophers described a concept known as the telos of an organism. The telos of something is the end at which it aims. The telos of an acorn, for example, is to become an oak tree. Acorns do not become chipmunks or rabbits. If conditions are favorable, they become what they are meant to be: oak trees. According to Aristotle, every organism has a telos that is intimately bound up with its nature in order that things become what they are meant to be.

Another way to say it is that a telos is a final cause of something. The telos or final cause of medicine is health. The telos or final cause of education is knowledge. In experiential education, each organization has a telos as well. It is essential to carefully examine that telos as part of our evaluation of the ethically tolerable accident.

In our earlier piloting example, the telos of commercial airline travel is safe delivery to a destination. The telos of the military, on the other hand, is to win wars. The military fighter pilot, therefore, accepts a different level of risk than the airline pilot does, even though the two perform many of the same activities. It is common knowledge that pilots who fly high performance fighter jets accept certain risks just by flying these aircraft. An F-16 is more dangerous than a 727 because the F-16 has been designed to achieve the telos of a combat mission. One carries weapons. The other carries passengers. One plane is highly temperamental to fly and the other is more predictable. The planes are different, the missions are different, and the teleologies are different. Therefore, the tolerability of risk differs between the two types of flying.

The same can be said of wilderness-based educational programs. The most basic question program managers and instructors must ask themselves is "Why am I doing what I am doing?" or "What is my telos?" The tolerability of risk will largely be ascertained by the answers given to these most basic questions.

As an example, let's compare the ethically tolerable amount of risk between two different organizations. I will call one organization the Oak Creek Outdoor School and the other the Cedar Creek Outdoor School. Let's say that I am a parent and I want to know about the difference between these two schools. Of course there will be some obvious differences: location, price, course schedule, staffing policies, etc. There may be many similarities between the two as well. However, as a parent, one of my main concerns is about the levels of risk my children will be exposed to; in other words, the acceptability of risk to me as a parent is of vital importance. Adults who are deciding whether to attend one school over another themselves are also interested in how much risk the organization finds acceptable. I think part of the answer lies in the teleologies of the two schools. Are the teleologies the same or are they different?

For the sake of our example, let's say the telos of the Oak Creek school is to teach certain character traits or "core values" to participants, including courage, physical fitness, compassion, and craftsmanship. The telos of the Cedar Creek school, on the other hand, is to develop outdoor leadership in extreme wilderness environments. Clearly, the teleologies are different, but what does this difference have to do with the acceptability of risk?

We'll take Oak Creek first. This school believes it is possible to teach courage, compassion, physical fitness, and craftsmanship while at the same time minimizing danger and risk to participants. A quote from the school's course catalog is very revealing.

> *Oak Creek Outdoor School is vitally concerned about the safety and welfare of its students. In fact your safety is the ultimate, most important value we hold. Our instructors use* perceived *risk as the vehicle by which we teach our core values. You can rest assured that the risks you encounter while here are more perceived than real. In fact our instructors are experts at setting up perceived risky experiences, while at the same time maintaining your safety. Our equipment is first rate and meets or exceeds industry standards for student safety and welfare.*

It is clear from this quote that Oak Creek's goal is to teach the specified core values using a wilderness setting but at the same time minimizing risk. In fact, the position is taken that safety is the "ultimate, most important value" of instructors. On empirical grounds it seems that the school has been successful in its approach, teaching the character values it espouses while at the same time running courses that are only perceptually risky. Real risk has been minimized, maybe even eliminated for all practical purposes. Therefore, it would be hard to ethically justify injecting risk—real risk as opposed to merely perceptual risk—into the programming of this school. Indeed, given the standards put forth in the catalog, it could be argued that no accident would be ethically tolerable for this particular wilderness-based program.

For a very different perspective, let's take a look at Cedar Creek's catalog. The Cedar Creek Outdoor School describes its telos as teaching leadership and teamwork, environmental studies, outdoor skills, and safety and judgment. In their statement about safety in wilderness programming, the school has this to say:

> *Wilderness activity involves hazards: rockfall, wild rivers, and freezing temperatures can pose a risk to even the most experienced outdoor leader. Activities ranging from simple day hikes to climbing glaciers can, due to errors in judgment or the unpredictable forces of nature, become dangerous and potentially life threatening .... It is important you understand that there are risks. Some adventure programs say that they can guarantee your safety. Cedar Creek Outdoor School does not. The risk of injury, even serious injury or death, is unavoidable in the outdoor environment in which we teach.*

It seems clear from this statement that the Cedar Creek Outdoor School accepts and even advertises to potential students the fact that they will be exposed to real and not merely perceived risk while on a course. Given that its aim includes the teaching of leadership, outdoor skills, and judgment, the institution has concluded that it would be inconsistent with its telos to attempt only risk-free activities or to design courses around merely perceived risks.

One would be hard pressed to find two more divergent views on the tolerability of risk than we find between Oak Creek and Cedar Creek. Indeed, my analysis suggests that Oak Creek Outdoor School is, in fact, risk averse, while Cedar Creek accepts the reality and tolerability of risk. My point is not to make a moral judgment here about the positions taken by the different schools. It is simply to point out the connection between divergent teleologies and different tolerances of risk. It appears that Oak Creek has decided its mission can be accomplished with very little real risk and that Cedar Creek has concluded the opposite: Its mission can't be carried on without it.

This comparison leads directly into the central issue of this chapter. Whether or not an accident is ethically tolerable must be determined within the context of the telos of the institution involved. This does not mean that we leap to conclusions and say that on an Oak Creek course absolutely no risk is acceptable (although one has to wonder, given the wording in their catalog). Nor does it mean that students on a Cedar Creek course will be lucky to come out alive. It does mean, however, that instructors in the field who have the ultimate responsibility for making decisions about safety and risk had better be very clear in their own minds about the telos of the organization for which they work and had better make decisions with that telos in mind.

I mentioned earlier the hypothetical instructor who decides to take a more risky route simply because he or she is bored with the standard route. Let's say that same thing happens in each of the two schools in our example. The instructor who works for Oak Creek, remember, is there to teach the goals of the Oak Creek school. It has been determined through past experience that a certain route on a given peak is an appropriate activity at this point in the course to accomplish at least part of the Oak Creek's telos. The instructor, however, is bored with this route. He or she elects to take the students on a more inherently risky route, one with greater real, not merely perceived, risks. An accident happens on the climb. Is this an "ethically tolerable" accident? My answer is no. Absent mitigating circumstances, such an accident would not be ethically tolerable.

Suppose the instructor worked for Cedar Creek instead. It may well be that the standard route, with its attendant low risk, is sufficiently difficult for teaching basic mountaineering leadership skills to a beginning Cedar Creek student. Granted, this venue might not be challenging enough for an advanced Cedar Creek student. But if the route was sufficient for the teaching of basic leadership, and the Cedar Creek instructor, bored, was to take the riskier route with no justified gain to a basic student, then that instructor would have the same ethical burden that the Oak Creek instructor has.

However, here is where a major divergence might take place, based on the different teleologies of the two schools. It is a fairly well established truth in mountaineering and technical rock climbing that instructors must be able to lead at a higher level than the routes they take students on. So, if a leader takes students on routes of, say, 5.5, then he or she should be capable of leading routes of 5.6-5.7 and so on. A strong argument can be made that Cedar Creek is obligated (by virtue of its telos) to impel its students to attempt climbs of a more difficult grade than the standard routes which they might be leading in the future. In other words, if an accident happened to a Cedar Creek student who was pushing his or her limits in order to accomplish the telos of leadership—again, absent mitigating circumstances—that accident might be ethically tolerable within that institution.

Hubris and the Acceptability of Risk

There is another concept from the ancient Greeks that is useful in analyzing the tolerability of accidents in the outdoors. *Hubris* refers to overbearing pride, presumption, or arrogance in a person's character. As I look back over the multitude of accidents that I am familiar with, there is a common theme in many of them that relates directly to the concept of hubris.

I was reading a book recently about the 1996 disaster on Mt. Everest, and I was struck by the way the author described the South Col route up the mountain as "the yak route." That phrase stopped me in my tracks. As I thought back to the climbers who first put in that route and the many people who have died or suffered on it, I could only shake my head in bewilderment and astonishment. How could any climber refer to any route up Everest as a "yak route?"

And yet they do. The same thing happens on other mountains, rivers, canyons, and other venues in wilderness settings as well. Trips and efforts that were historically challenging and even dangerous become trivialized and are even treated with contempt by certain people who have developed an attitude of arrogance and pride towards these settings. It is my position that there is no such thing as a "safe" route up Everest—or Mt. Rainier, for that matter. The same holds for virtually every other wilderness environment in which we operate.

Hubris occurs when people begin to lose the respect they once had for the dangers and seriousness of wilderness areas. This usually happens because of their past successes in these areas or because they have developed personal skills that are higher than the skills needed on past endeavors. What was once personally challenging becomes routine, even boring. However, the potential for an accident is just as real on the 100th ascent as it was on the first ascent. Failure to recognize this fact is an act of hubris that can lead to disaster.

Once again, I am impressed by aircraft pilots and their institutionalized respect for what they do. They go through their preflight safety checklists, whether they have 100 hours or 10,000 hours of experience. Pilots who neglect the basics are considered inherently dangerous in the flying world. The same is, or ought to be, true of instructors and leaders in wilderness-based education. Hubris is an unnecessary, and intolerable, risk.

The potential for an accident is just as real on the 100th ascent as it was on the first ascent.

When we consider the tolerability of a given accident, we need to look for examples of hubris. Was this accident caused at least partially by an attitude of arrogance, undue pride, or presumptuousness on the part of the leader(s)? If it was, then the accident becomes ethically problematic, even intolerable. If a given venue caused a person to approach it with caution, care, even fear the first time around, then I suggest that same humility is appropriate and that same caution should be exercised on the 100th use of that venue, too. If a wilderness-based educator loses that respect, then it is arguable that he or she should not be leading students in that setting any more. In a wilderness context, lack of respect towards that which at one time evoked respect (or even fear) is a warning sign of approaching hubris.

A Cultural Gap

Often there is a cultural gap between the people who do wilderness programming for a living and those who come on courses. Over the years, I have been struck by the insularity of many wilderness education professionals and the gap that separates them from the rest of society. Many wilderness professionals embrace a "counter culture" lifestyle that is at odds with the norms of the majority and many of the minority cultures in America.

For instance, there may be a great variance between the level of risk outdoor educators find acceptable as compared to the level that students find acceptable. Students do not always realize the amount of risk they are being exposed to. It has been my experience that a vast number of Americans do not have a clue about the potential risks that are inherent in wilderness activities. Evidence for this can be seen in something as seemingly minor as the kind of gear people wear in rainy weather. Professionals tend to choose gear that will prevent hypothermia after prolonged exposure to rain, wind, and cold. Non-professionals often pay attention to different features such as color and style, how something looks and whether or not it goes with another thing. They do not always understand that the risk of hypothermia is real.

The greater the cultural and lifestyle gap between professionals and their students or clients, the greater the potential for placing people in inappropriately risky situations.

I think it is advisable for professionals in wilderness education to be aware of this issue and how it might influence their decisions on the acceptability of risk. The greater the cultural and lifestyle gap between professionals and their students or clients, the greater the potential for placing people in inappropriately risky situations. It is very easy for those who do risky activities for a living to grant a level of ethical acceptability or tolerability to accidents that might not be even remotely shared by the broader public. I suggest a very careful, ongoing, critical self-reflection on the part of wilderness educators in this area.

Informed Consent: An Ethical Imperative

The discussion about the ethical acceptability of risk and the telos of an organization was framed earlier in terms of course catalogs and other program publications. But it does not follow that, just because I have read a statement describing the telos of an organization or program, I am therefore adequately informed about the risks associated with attempting to achieve that telos. A fuller understanding rests on the foundational concept of informed consent.

Informed consent is both a legal and an ethical imperative. The legal perspective is discussed more thoroughly in Chapter Four, particularly in regard to the wording and presentation of release forms. From an ethical standpoint, however, the more completely a participant has been informed about risks, the better able he or she is to agree to accept those risks. And the more a participant fully understands and accepts the risks he or she is agreeing to, the more ethically justified the program is in using greater risks.

Students of the Greek philosopher Plato are familiar with the paradox of the impossibility of attaining knowledge. Basically the argument goes like this. Either one knows or one does not know. If one knows, then why would one seek to know what one knows, since one already knows it? On the other hand, if one does not know, then how can one seek to know what one does not know? Due to one's ignorance, one would not even know what to look for. Indeed, if one does not know but then attains knowledge, how would one know one had attained knowledge or falsehood? One does not know the difference between the two, since one starts from ignorance!

This is the sort of puzzle that drives non-philosophers crazy, but I think it is useful for the issue of informed consent. Put simply, the question is this: How can I give informed consent to risks that I do not know about until I have encountered them? In other words, doesn't informed consent imply that I have knowledge of that in which I am about to become involved? However, I have not yet gotten involved, so how can my consent possibly be informed?

Modern philosopher John Dewey provides an answer to the old problem posed by Plato. Dewey argues that the paradox rests on an assumption that knowledge is an all or nothing affair. This assumption fails to account for the process of coming to know. Dewey argues that in reality human beings acquire knowledge gradually and in a processive manner. Coming to know is not a condition of either/or; instead it is incremental, processive, and gradual.

As a practical matter, risk management practitioners have something to learn from both of these great philosophers. Plato raises a vital question about the difficulty of knowledge. When we say that we are informing our students or clients about risks, then we are operating in the knowledge arena, not as a theoretical matter for a philosophy seminar, but as a matter of life, death, or injury for those who come to our programs. Yet Dewey's reply provides a practical "solution." We should see informed consent as a gradual, on-going matter that pervades the entire relationship we have with students or clients.

I remember hearing an experienced medical doctor talk about informed consent between patients and physicians.

Speaking from a medical ethics standpoint, he said that the most common mistake health care professionals make regarding informed consent is to assume that once a patient has signed a release the matter is closed. Too often, once the form has been signed, health care providers never ask for informed consent again. His point was that health care providers should be getting informed consent regularly from their patients, throughout the entire professional relationship.

None of our potential students or clients is either completely knowledgeable or completely ignorant about potential risks in wilderness education. Rather, each of them lies somewhere along a continuum between the two extremes. The problem for the ethically concerned practitioner is to determine where along that continuum a particular individual lies. A reasonable man or woman is only able to make a truly informed consent decision relative to the place he or she occupies on the knowledge-ignorance continuum.

In the legal arena, informed consent is related to what a "reasonable man or woman" might think or do. This issue is complicated by the fact that there is no absolute standard of reasonableness. Any number of parties may be called upon to make a determination of reasonableness, including individuals, program administrators, outside agencies, professional certification and licensing agencies, and judges or jurors in a legal proceeding. It is beyond the scope of this chapter to attempt a definition of what a reasonable informed consent might be. However, it is sufficient at this point to be aware that the concept exists, that it affects the determination of informed consent, and that an ethical organization needs therefore to consider it when designing its approach to risk management.

Another ethical problem can occur whenever there is a gap between an organization's marketing and admission departments and what actually goes on in the field. Several years ago I was speaking at a well-known outdoor education school. It was the all-staff meeting, just before the summer season with students got underway. The issue of acceptable risk came up. I asked the assembled field instructors how many of them had read the material that their students had been sent by the marketing and admissions departments. Out of some 95 field instructors, not one had read the most recent material that had gone out to students. The office staff who were there were quite taken aback. The point is that it is extremely easy for a gap like this to develop between field staff and office staff, and for the perception of risk to be different on either side of that gap.

A different problem can occur when an organization paints a too-rosy picture of itself to the public. I am grateful to Mr. Charles (Reb) Gregg, LL.B., an attorney active in legal issues in outdoor education, who pointed out the significance (both legally and ethically) of the kinds of photographs that an institution puts in its public catalogs. If the photographs depict only happy, smiling people in safe situations, he noted, then potential students might well get a false impression of what they are really getting themselves into. It is arguable that the pictures in an organization's catalog should accurately reflect the potential risks and hazards students or clients might encounter on the institution's outings. This point has tremendous implications for the ethics of informed consent.

Marketing and admissions departments, of course, are often under extreme pressure to fill courses. After all, that is what they are hired to do. Thus a tension can develop between the ethically concerned practitioner who wants to adequately inform potential students and clients about the risks of a particular course or program and the equally ethically concerned, yet market driven, admissions and marketing people who do not want to scare potential students away. At minimum, the field staff and the admissions and marketing staffs need to be in close communication about the potential risks inherent in the programming offered by the school. From an ethical perspective, it is better to overplay the potential risks involved in the interests of informed consent than to underplay them in the interests of enrollment.

In summary, I would like to make four practical suggestions for outdoor professionals to consider. First, program marketing materials and any other informational publications that discuss risks must do so in terms of the telos of the organization. Second, risk managers must make a good faith effort to understand how much potential students or clients really know or do not know regarding what they are getting themselves into when they come on programs involving wilderness-based risks. Third, informed consent must be seen as an ongoing ethical obligation throughout the entire duration of the professional relationship. Informed consent is not a one-time responsibility, completed through pre-course materials and documents, and then forgotten. Instead, field instructors should regularly discuss risks with their students and re-obtain their consent on an ongoing basis. And finally, the standard of the "reasonable man or woman" should govern this exchange between information and consent in wilderness-based professional relationships.

Ethical Feedback Loops

I can remember my time as a field instructor for two Outward Bound schools: North Carolina and Pacific Crest. One of the key things I learned from Outward Bound was the importance of external safety reviews, conducted by evaluators from other Outward Bound schools. We would be out in the field, on course, and a safety review team would suddenly appear and just watch what I was doing with my students. Similar reviews were conducted throughout the school's entire programming. Each review team produced a report reflecting on what they had observed. The entire school would then use that review as a source for reflection and learning in areas of safety and risk management. In other words, Outward Bound built in risk management feedback loops for their entire system. Many people would argue that they set a standard for safety reviews that has become a de facto industry standard.

Drawing from this precedent, I think it is useful for all outdoor education schools to develop ethical feedback loops. An ethical feedback loop is any means whereby an organization regularly engages in ethical analysis and reflection and then acts on those insights. Too often, ethical reflection only occurs after some sort of problem has arisen. But it doesn't have to be that way. Regular ethical reflection can be as integral to an organization's functioning as accounting or equipment inventories. This means institutionalizing ethics as a mainstream concern at all levels of the organization. Field staff, office staff, members of the board of trustees, every member of the organization can and should engage in ethical reflection. I am not suggesting some sort of prissy puritanism here whereby institutions suffer from the "paralysis of analysis" and ethics becomes an undue burden. Rather, I am suggesting the inclusion of ethics within the overall context of the organization and its mission. I urge practitioners to take a proactive rather than a reactive approach to these issues.

An Ethically Tolerable Accident?

I want to take my final pages to connect the history and telos of the Wilderness Risk Management Conference with the topic I've been discussing throughout this chapter. Since the mid- to late 1980s, there has been an ongoing discussion within the National Outdoor Leadership School (NOLS) about the broader issue of safety and risk management at the national level, issues that affect other outdoor programs besides just NOLS. I can remember participating in the end-of-season NOLS staff conferences in Lander, Wyoming, during the early years of those discussions. Seminars were offered. Speakers came in from other programs. Intense discussions were held about wilderness programming, safety, risk management, and a host of other topics. The NOLS leadership wanted their staff to have an opportunity to learn from each other and from other professionals so that their own professionalism would be enhanced, with the concomitant result of better courses for their future students. There was also a desire from NOLS that there be more open discussion about risk within the profession of outdoor education.

Also in the late1980s, three NOLS students and one instructor attempted to climb Mt. Warren in the Wind River Range of Wyoming. During the ascent, the weather deteriorated and time was running out, so the instructor decided to abandon the summit bid and descend from the peak. As part of the descent, the instructor decided to lower the students over some steep rock to a snow couloir and then exit the mountain via the couloir and an adjoining glacier. The instructor was careful to make sure that once a student had been lowered there was sufficient space on the resting ledge for the student to move well out of the way of the fall line of the next descending student. It is an accepted mountaineering practice to avoid standing beneath people who are rappelling or being lowered, due to the possibility that the person descending might dislodge a rock that could injure the climber below.

The first student, 24-year-old David Black, was lowered to the ledge. There was a large-enough space to clear the fall line of the other descending students. The second student was also lowered without incident. The third student, however, accidentally dislodged a rock the size of a small watermelon. The rock ricocheted off the wall and struck David Black's helmet, even though David was well out of the way of the natural fall line of the lower/rappel system. David Black died from injuries received in this accident.

One of the hallmarks of the ethically tolerable accident is the accident that helps in the development of meaning for people.

A post-accident investigation and analysis determined that the accident was caused by a freak ricochet and that the instructor and students involved had operated well within the standards of prudent mountaineers with their level of experience and training for the activity they were engaged in. However, that was not the end of the story.

David Black's family was in severe grief and searching for some meaning in their son's death. The NOLS community was also in grief and also sought meaning in this tragedy. What happened next makes profound ethical sense. The combined sorrow and grief brought David Black's family and the NOLS organization together in a creative and ethically acceptable way. Rather than engage in blame, accusation, and retribution for this event, the family and the outdoor leadership school came together to find a mutually beneficial meaning and resolution.

David's parents wanted his death to help produce something useful for the profession of wilderness education. They did not want him to have died in vain. I do not have the space here to go into the details, but the death of David Black coincided with the prior efforts of NOLS to get a national dialogue going about risk management and led to the creation of The Wilderness Risk Managers' Committee and the first national Wilderness Risk Management Conference in 1994. The committee and conference had been envisioned before, but David Black's death was a catalyst that helped in overcoming lingering inertia and getting the ball rolling. Other major players in the wilderness education field (such as Outward Bound, the American Alpine Club, Student Conservation Association, Wilderness Medical Society, and the Boy Scouts) came on board to aid the National Outdoor Leadership School in its efforts to encourage a national and international dialogue about risk management issues.

Recall that I suggested in the opening of this chapter that the ethically unacceptable, intolerable accident was one that is not discussed openly, not learned from, not used as a teaching vehicle for practitioners as they go about their professional lives in the future. Human beings by their very nature seek meaning out of life. We can stand great tragedy, great loss, and great suffering. But we have a very low tolerance for the loss of meaning, for meaninglessness. One of the hallmarks of the ethically tolerable accident, in my view, is the accident that helps in the development of meaning for people. It is not caused by negligence, boredom, arrogance, or any of the other questionable practices outlined here. An accident that might be deemed tolerable is one not caused by negligence and from which great learning takes place, where people think about things they may not have thought about before, where the balance between risk and benefit is examined, where the continued welfare of our students is held as a sacred trust.

> An accident that might be deemed tolerable is one from which great learning takes place, where people think about things they may not have thought about before.

When we engage each other in dialogue, in argument, in the sharing of the latest research, and informal discussion, we are well on the way to creating meaning. As I think about Willi Unsoeld and Devi Unsoeld and Brad Shaver and Scott Fischer and David Black and all the others who have died or been injured in wilderness accidents, I realize we have a moral, ethical obligation to learn and to share our learning, drawing from their experiences and from our own.

Facing these difficult issues openly and honestly together is at least a step in the right direction toward understanding the ethical foundations of wilderness-based risk management.

The Importance of Ongoing Assessment

By William L. Ennis and Constance E. Livsey © 2000

Chapter Seven uses a case study to emphasize the evolution all long-standing outdoor agencies inevitably undergo over time. These changes, which can be very gradual, may result in significant alteration to the nature of an organization and can ultimately affect the potential for an accident. The authors, long-time instructors for a university outdoor department, provide personal insight and perspective into how these changes might have helped set the stage for an accident that occurred in their program in 1997, and they believe that a better assessment process may have reduced the

Change is inevitable, and longstanding outdoor programs are not immune to this reality. Over time, managers or owners, instructors, and clientele will come and go. Even program philosophy may evolve. This evolution, which can occur quite gradually and escape notice over the short term, can ultimately result in an insidious but significant alteration to the nature and safety of an organization. Unfortunately, it often takes a serious or fatal accident before an in-depth and sometimes painful self-examination takes place, and it is only in hindsight that the obvious becomes clear.

Using the University of Alaska Anchorage (UAA) outdoor program as a case study, this chapter examines changes that can potentially occur in any outdoor program. While these changes in external structure, clientele, goals, and philosophy were not directly responsible for UAA's accident on

Ptarmigan Peak, we believe they may have set the stage for an incident to occur. It is our hope that other outdoor programs can learn from this experience and take steps to critically and honestly evaluate all aspects their own organizations—*before* the next accident happens.

The Evolution of an Outdoor Program

The University of Alaska Anchorage's outdoor education program had its beginnings in courses taught in the Anchorage Community College (ACC). In the 1970s, ACC was a thriving and popular community college, providing the people of Anchorage with general-education, job-training, and personal-enrichment courses. The economy was booming, and people from all over the country were lured north by the high salaries and many available opportunities, particularly in natural resource development. Young engineers, attorneys, and other skilled and well-paid workers moved to the state, most of them eager to immerse themselves in Alaska and the opportunities it offered. Consequently, ACC's student population consisted largely of professional adults who were new to Alaska, many of whom wished to learn technical outdoor skills.

It was during this time and within this community that ACC's original mountaineering course was introduced. The first instructor of mountaineering was a sociology professor (and avid climber) who taught the rudiments of the activity to a generation of local adults. He later went on to create and teach courses in winter survival, backpacking, and intermediate mountaineering, and to lead a number of expeditions throughout the United States and South America. Eventually these courses were housed in a department called Alaska Wilderness Studies, or AWS.

Even as the department grew, two main faculty members provided nearly all instruction in the program. Although the mountaineering classes were the core of AWS, the curriculum grew steadily until the department offered a wide range of content. The management style of the program in those early years was aggressively hands-off. Paperwork was minimal, and field manuals non-existent. The tiny AWS office was crammed with an assortment of equipment and climbing hardware because storage space was inadequate. Though the

ACC administration did not necessarily embrace the courses, it permitted them to be offered because of the community interest and support they drew.

In the early days of AWS, students were educated largely through full immersion in the outdoor activity. Lacking field manuals, course content guides, and formal pedagogical policies, the program educated its students through a truly experience-based, hands-on approach. It was not unheard of, for instance, for a student to be handed a rack of rock climbing hardware (with little additional instruction) and asked to lead a route. Students who were uncomfortable with this approach withdrew from the course. The ones who accepted the program's adventurous philosophy continued.

Over time, AWS developed a reputation in the community for providing students with a solid foundation in climbing skills, and the classes were not considered a hospitable learning environment for the timid. Weekend outings generally began with the instructors and participants meeting for breakfast, where the climbing venue would be determined on the spot (based on weather and snow conditions). On Saturday, the approach hike was followed by a field session on the topic of instruction for the day. Sunday would start with an early morning wake-up call, followed by a rigorous and challenging climb that sometimes lasted late into the night. Outings often ended over pizzas and beer. The camaraderie that developed led to many life-long friendships and a surprising number of marriages.

The AWS instructional model, which seemed to place "adventure" ahead of "education," was nonetheless remarkably successful in that it was extremely popular and relatively accident-free. Mountaineering class sizes averaged a now-unthinkable 30 to 35 students, and waiting lists for enrollment were the norm. The courses were physically and mentally demanding, and one that started with 35 students usually ended with only a dozen participants.

Students acquired a solid base of skills from each other and from their instructors. The breathtaking beauty of Alaska, the exhilarating nature of climbing, the joyful camaraderie, and the charisma of risk-taking personalities were powerful incentives to continue mountaineering and support the department. Serious injuries were rare, and most incidents consisted of a broken bone, twisted knee, or other non-dramatic damage. AWS "graduates" filtered into every part of the local outdoor community. They appeared as sales staff in equipment stores, apprentice guides, and mountaineering clients (and even guides) in many parts of the world. AWS produced competent climbers, many of whom continued their pursuits as serious amateurs and even professionals.

The department's approach, and particularly its emphasis on technical skills, was not necessarily academic in the traditional sense, but it served the needs of its clients well.

The department's approach, and particularly its emphasis on technical skills, was not necessarily academic in the traditional sense, but it served the needs of its clients well. Because its "students" were older adults who had significant amounts of outdoor experience, the program assumed (with little problem) that its client base had a good understanding of the inherent risks associated with outdoor activities. Consequently, little time was spent formally educating them on course expectations, goals and outcomes, or on obtaining informed consent in writing. These assumptions remained in place long after the AWS program had gradually outgrown them.

Although many of the department's courses were offered for college credit, in essence AWS more closely resembled a college outing club than an academic program. Similar to other outdoor programs at the time, the department operated without rigid operational procedures, and it was not overly concerned about the lack of pedagogy and sequential-learning emphasis that is provided today. Today's university outdoor education programs generally place less emphasis on "building mountaineers" and more typically introduce students to various outdoor activities while incorporating a minimal amount of actual risk.

While the outing-club model of instruction would never be approved in the traditional academic setting in which the department now operates, it made sense at the time. The program was a visible and established part of Anchorage's outdoor and mountaineering community. The program's reputation helped filter incoming students who sought to gain outdoor skills in an adult-education setting. They brought with them self-reliance, a sense of responsibility, and a willingness to accept a level of risk consistent with climbing and traveling in Alaska's often-unforgiving backcountry environment. And though some of the methods used may have been informal (such as the breakfast and dinner briefing and debriefing sessions), they served their purpose: Students were educated about risks and expectations; time was spent on reflection and developing judgment; and personal growth was encouraged, albeit indirectly.

In summary, the success of the AWS program of the 1970s and 1980s reflected the extent to which the goals of the program's management and leadership matched the expectations of its clientele. At every level of the department's structure—coordinator, instructors, and participants—there was agreement as to its purpose. There was little overt pressure from the administration to alter either the program's course offerings or its adventure-based approach to teaching the subject matter. Additionally, there was solid agreement among instructional staff and students as to what was being offered: instruction in technical skills with an emphasis on real-world outdoor experience. The program's educators were not only friends and avid climbers, they embraced the AWS mission: to teach technical outdoor skills to a population of eager adult participants. In terms of the department's structure and function, it was a period of unparalleled harmony between the community-education-based mission of ACC, the philosophy of the AWS leadership, and the desires and expectations of the people taking the courses.

The program's design, however, was one that would gradually become outmoded before anyone in the program realized the need for policy assessment and change.

With Time Comes Change

Nothing lasts forever, and by the mid-1980s Alaska's economic boom appeared to be waning. The downturn in the economy forced the University of Alaska to evaluate its structure and operating expenses, and in 1987 it was announced that the state's universities and community colleges would merge and be based out of three major centers; Anchorage, Fairbanks and Juneau. During this process, ACC lost its status as a separate college and was absorbed into the newly created University of Alaska Anchorage (UAA).

That change, in turn, introduced considerable turmoil into the AWS program. The department coordinator realized that AWS's mission was not necessarily in sync with UAA's mission, and the program was an anathema to the university's administration. He acknowledged that some modification to the department's established goal of teaching technical outdoor skills in a field-based setting would almost inevitably be necessary. However, his suggestion that the department change its focus (and in effect its mission), was not necessarily welcomed by all. A core group of long-term instructors and dedicated volunteers wanted to continue offering what they felt was an important, marketable skill set. Others, including the coordinator and some of the newer instructors, saw a need for compromise in order to fit in with the changing times. AWS was faced with the unwelcome evolutionary pressures that come with time.

AWS was faced with the unwelcome evolutionary pressures that come with time.

A Change in Mission

The department found itself in the precarious position of being a university-based program that functioned (more or less) as an informal outing club. Many of its strong traditions now became liabilities. Not only was the department's mission in conflict with the university's mission, the merger resulted in traditional college-age students (who had a different set of expectations) enrolling for courses. The community, too, had a different expectation of what should be included in a public, university-based outdoor program. Although the department and its followers believed strongly in the need to allow participants to experience actual risk, it was a mind-set that was at odds with many traditional students and with community members at large.

As a result, an impasse arose regarding the basic nature of AWS's courses. Although experiential education was beginning to stand on its own feet, there were only a few successful and well-known models or "peer institutes," such as the National Outdoor Leadership School (NOLS) and Outward Bound. Yet these programs differed from AWS in many ways. Neither, for example, is housed within a public university. Further, NOLS is able to provide technical outdoor skills in 30- to 45- day expeditions, a setup not conducive to traditional students or a university setting. Outward Bound, on the other hand, uses adventure as the catalyst for personal growth: It is not that program's purpose to teach technical skills. The coordinator ultimately saw the Outward Bound model as the one most in line with AWS's future. This belief prompted him to try to move AWS away from emphasizing technical skills (and inherent, actual risk) and into a safer, "personal growth" model.

Not surprisingly, these changes evoked passionate debates over the department's mission and identity. There was fierce resistance from some of the program's instructors and volunteers, and several experienced and well-regarded instructors quit as a result. The level of conflict and "disconnect" between the goals and expectations, within the program as well as with the university's administration, was clearly evident yet remained unresolved. Rather than address the issue thoroughly to make sure everyone understood and accepted this change in mission and philosophy, the program simply continued to evolve, with the interpretation of these changes left to the individual: The program director saw the department as needing to become more academic in order to fit in with the university; the students saw the courses as interesting physical education credits (in fact, the program became part of a Health, Outdoor, and Physical Education degree); and each instructor was left to make his or her own determination about the program's mission, philosophy, and the level of risk that students should face in the field.

New Instructors

Instructor selection had never been much of an issue for AWS in the 1970s and 1980s. Instructors and assistants were typically well known by the coordinator and hired on the basis of that personal knowledge. Often, volunteers would be "groomed" into a paid position once they had put in their time and accumulated enough experience. For instance, volunteers often attended evening lab sessions and climbing weekends and acted as rope-team leaders and advisors. The students looked up to them for their experience and benefited greatly from their enthusiasm and willingness to pass on knowledge. Although the volunteers received no pay, they received that certain kind of glory afforded by beginners to "real climbers," and they were able to develop judgment through the experience. An informal and unspoken mentoring program consequently existed throughout the 1980s and even into the very early 1990s: One took AWS courses, returned and served for several semesters as a volunteer, and eventually a paid assistant position would likely be offered.

This hiring strategy, de facto apprenticeship program, and feedback loop proved effective for nearly 20 years. The instructors used familiar routes with a known and acceptable level of risk. They would get together and discuss outings, equipment needs and concerns, personnel issues, and plans for the future. Long-term volunteers and field assistants often joined the discussions and were relied upon for their perceptions of students' progress and the program's success and safety. This system of information transfer was quite effective in maintaining continuity of course content, teaching style, and risk management. Indeed, in the early 1990s, the program was evaluated by local outdoors experts who stated that the senior instructors and instructor longevity were among the program's greatest strengths.

AWS's practice of grooming and selecting its instructors and paid field assistants from within, and its tradition of retaining the same instructors over the long-term, were markedly different from the practices often employed today. Today's outdoor agencies, instead, often select instructors on a course-by-course or semester-by-semester basis from a large pool of applicants. Although many organizations across the country practiced hiring methods similar to AWS's in the 1970s and 1980s, the exponential growth of both users and instructors in the outdoor education industry has made it difficult for agencies to retain staff over the years. Although the same is true of UAA's outdoor department today, AWS lagged behind other organizations and did not experience this change as early as its Lower 48 counterparts.

In the 1990s, the national trend caught up with AWS, and changing mechanics of instructor selection began to affect the department. Because more and more courses were being offered, there were not enough experienced people available to teach them or mentor the new instructors. It was known that the long-term educators would eventually retire, and new instructors would be needed to replace them. Further, because many of the department's students were now "traditional," few had an interest in becoming (or were qualified to be hired as) an instructor, and the department's volunteer apprentice program evaporated.

To meet these demands for a broader instructor pool, the coordinator began to hire instructors who were not intimately familiar with the program. He also began to make hiring decisions for field assistants without input from the course instructors, and with increasing frequency, instructors did not know the people with whom they would be working. In this fashion, AWS's traditional methods for ensuring continuity of teaching style, course content, and risk assessment among the instructional team were disrupted. The process for transferring information (through longevity and apprenticeships) was gone, and no formal system had been created to replace it.

Some sort of guidelines would be needed if new employees, unfamiliar with the program's philosophy and methods, were to be utilized.

As a result, and not surprisingly, problems arose. Some of the newly hired instructors had spent limited time in Alaska's backcountry, and consequently lacked essential experience upon which to base their decisions. Further, because new educators were unfamiliar with the way a course had been taught previously, instructors often defined their own curricula and made their own decisions about what should be offered in a class. Formal course content guides existed for some courses, but in many cases instructors were not required to use them.

The program also lacked a formal field manual containing information as to appropriate venues, routes, and accepted field practices. During the construction of the first of several field manuals, some of the instructors chanted "rules are for fools." While this view may be common among climbers and may have been perfectly valid in the early years of AWS, it did not reflect the realities of the new approach to instructor hiring. Some sort of guidelines would be needed if new employees, unfamiliar with the program's philosophy and methods, were to be utilized. Further, the intimate feedback loops that had previously carried so much important information back and forth were no longer effective. The program's traditionally informal climate, once its greatest asset, was becoming outmoded.

Throughout this evolution, frustration mounted. Established instructors did not always feel the newer employees were qualified to teach the courses. For the most part, the circle of experienced AWS instructors was reluctant to accept people from outside the program, and new instructors did not feel welcomed. Although most people acknowledged the mounting challenges, little was done to effectively address or fix the predicament.

A New Clientele

AWS's clientele did not immediately shift with any of the department's mergers or changes in the local economy. Instead, the process was gradual. Over time, classes were filling with fewer professionals and more traditional college students in the 18- to 24-year-old age bracket. Not only did their backgrounds differ, but the new clients also expected a different sort of educational experience. For instance, it was not uncommon for the 1990s students to want to return home early on Sunday in order to study for other classes. In one instance, a student was horrified to learn that the group was actually going to go into the mountains while it was snowing. There were other examples of students not bringing additional warm clothing on weekend field sessions in order to leave room in their packs for textbooks.

Another difference was that this new generation of students was not necessarily dedicated to learning and loving the course material; in many cases, they were simply in search of a few "easy" college credits. More importantly, they often had little real world experience. Many had spent minimal time outdoors and had considerably less experience in making field decisions (with potentially serious consequences) than their predecessors had. They did not bring with them an appreciation of the inherent risks of climbing that previous students (professional adults) usually had, and they had fewer discretionary dollars for buying the necessary climbing or outdoor gear.

If this change in participant demographics had occurred overnight, the AWS program might have more easily and readily adapted, and the department might have recognized early on a need to reevaluate its mission, its pedagogy, and its safety standards. But the shift occurred slowly, one student at a time, and the program continued to treat its increasingly young, inexperienced clients like the more mature outdoor enthusiasts who had initially shaped its principles. Further, instructors were often slow to realize that these new clients expected a class to be similar in many ways to their other university courses. The new students expected AWS outings to be based on sequential development and an assessment of skills; they thought courses would be challenging yet inclusive and encouraging; and perhaps most importantly, they did not expect to be exposed to potentially perilous situations.

This change in student population, like the other changes noted earlier in this chapter, did not result in a dangerous program. Nonetheless, after the 1997 accident, the department more fully recognized that it was conducting its activities and treating its clients much the same as it had in the 1970s and 1980s. Although the student-base had evolved through time, the manner in which the program communicated with those students apparently had not.

If this change had occurred overnight, the program might have more easily and readily adapted. But the shift occurred slowly, one student at a time.

The Key to Ongoing Assessment

Trends in the evolution of any outdoor program will likely have a significant impact on a program's success or failure, and these trends and their consequences should be evaluated on an ongoing basis. The entire UAA program grew out of a single course taught by one individual. For many years, the program's philosophy and methods were quite successful; however, significant changes occurred through the years. It was not until recently that the department examined itself closely enough to recognize the degree to which these changes had affected its operation.

Each outdoor program has its own unique origin, history, and players. While few will be able to relate to the exact evolution that AWS experienced, many will be able to recognize how similar changes have affected their own organizations through the years. The following points, we believe, are fundamental to all outdoor agencies–no matter how large or small, young or established–and should be examined regularly.

Dialogue with Students

Every outdoor agency must ensure that a "disconnect" does not develop between the program's goals, mission and philosophies, and its students' or clients' acceptance and understanding of them. An agency, and all its employees, should have a clear understanding of how much risk is considered acceptable. Be willing to ask the following questions: What level of risk can a novice be expected to accept or even understand? When can a student decline to participate in or walk away from an activity? Should a student be expected to master skills to the extent that his or her safety or very survival depends on them? How much responsibility for safe practices can an instructor shift to students? Are there program guidelines for any of these decisions? As Jasper Hunt points out in Chapter Six, these questions, and a host of similar ones, should be at the very core of the every outdoor program, especially as its clientele expands.

An agency, and all its employees, should have a clear understanding of how much risk is considered acceptable.

Early in AWS's history, students knew what to expect before they ever enrolled in a course, or they learned very quickly thereafter. The program's reputation made it clear that climbs would be both physically and mentally demanding. Students enrolled precisely because they knew that the class would present them with difficult situations requiring skill mastery and physical endurance. There was an important, running dialogue between the instructors and the students on what each could expect. Although the process was informal, it effectively provided the foundation for "informed consent" that is so important to appropriate and ethical programming.

As the department evolved within a more formal academic setting, no single instrument was initiated to reproduce the communication with students that had existed through this informal process. In fact, it is possible that no one was fully aware of the passing of this crucial component. As the organization grew, it was slow to develop standardized strategies to ensure that many such practices, once offhand and assumed, were effectively and consistently occurring with the changing student population.

Instructor Dialogue and Feedback Loops

Most outdoor educators recognize the importance of

sharing information among instructors, whether it occurs on a mountain or in the office. Much can be learned from one another's experiences, and an agency that promotes open communication will certainly gain from the practice. Not only can instructors benefit from sharing techniques or close calls, a group's well-being will obviously be aided if instructors feel free to question or confront one another in the field. Consequently, it is essential that feedback loops—whether formal or informal—be used and maintained.

Not only can instructors benefit from sharing techniques or close calls, a group's well-being will obviously be aided if instructors feel free to question or confront one another in the field.

Early on, AWS had only a handful of instructors, all of whom were experienced local climbers and climbing friends. They went on outings together and spent time discussing their classes and goals. During AWS parties and other gatherings, the instructors would debrief a semester's courses, discuss accidents and incidents, exchange field information and mountaineering techniques, discuss equipment needs, and evaluate student progress. As the department grew, these gatherings became less frequent and much of this information transfer was lost.

It was not until recently that the department recognized how important this process was to AWS's programming. This feedback loop effectively transferred information from one instructor to another. Instructors were willing to pass along knowledge, learn from each other's successes and failures, and confront one another's decisions. When the instructor-hire methods changed, the department was challenged when it came to implementing a new system that would effectively maintain this process.

Interaction Between Staff and Management

A common problem within many organizations, especially large ones, is the poor communication that exists between field workers and administrators. Although policies and attitudes change through the years, the changes are often made at the management level, and the information does not effectively make it to the field instructor. Dialogue between staff and management, whether formal or informal, is critical if a program hopes to have clear roles and expectations, especially as they evolve over time.

Traditionally, all employees within the AWS organization understood and accepted the goals, safety standards, and philosophy of the program. An effective feedback loop (described earlier) was used to make sure field staff and administrators understood and were in agreement as to roles and responsibilities. The program emphasized technical skills, and each instructor was given free reign to accomplish this simple directive. This understanding was communicated in tents on mountains and through conversations in town.

Through the years, there were many changes within the department, yet no formal mechanism was incorporated to ensure that these changes were clearly addressed or understood by the ever-growing pool of instructors. When management and staff did communicate, the two sides did not always agree on the changes or about the direction that the program should be taking. Consequently, incomplete and ineffective dialogue often resulted.

Instructor Selection

Instructor selection (and longevity) seems to be a shared concern nationwide. With the trend toward an increasing number of people choosing to participate in the outdoors, the need for competent instructors is apparent and growing. Yet, in order to be an effective leader, one must first gain experience and judgment. The question becomes, *what does it take to be an effective outdoor leader, and how can an agency hold on to the competent leaders it employs?*

In the early years, AWS instructors were hired individually for the contribution each could make to a specific course. Each was handpicked from a pool of prospects by a coordinator who personally observed the potential employee's skills and judgment in the field. These new instructors knew the program's goals, knew how the material should be taught, knew the routes on each mountain, and ultimately had the experience to know when to retreat in the face of deteriorating weather or avalanche hazard.

Through the years, the need for ever greater numbers of educators and new types of courses outstripped the ability of the core leaders to fill positions or provide new candidates with the mentoring required. Although the department ultimately developed a formal process for identifying what qualities it looks for in a lead instructor (as discussed earlier in this book), it holds no magic wand for knowing how to keep those instructors long-term.

Conclusion

For two years after the accident, AWS engaged in an extensive process that included an accident investigation and a total reassessment of every aspect of the outdoor program. As is the case with accidents themselves (as discussed in Chapter One), it is rare that any one factor or event will cause an end result. Similarly, we believe that a combination of multiple factors (associated with the department's evolution) may have contributed to a potentially outdated system. Consequently, many changes were implemented (see Chapter Three). Although some of the original instructors chafed at the new paperwork, restrictions, and limitations, they acknowledged that many of the modifications were necessary and beneficial.

All organizations can gain from such in-depth self-assessment. The sad part is, many will wait until an accident before they take the time to look deep enough or with a sincere and critical eye. As is noted in Chapter Three, assessment is not about finding flaws; it is an indispensable tool for improvement.

All organizations can gain from in-depth self-assessment. The sad part is, many will wait until an accident before they take the time to look deep enough or with a sincere and critical eye.

The following list can be used as a roadmap for self-examination. In most cases, these issues have been addressed thoroughly elsewhere in this book.

- Always be aware of the big picture. This is especially important when your staff seems most involved in internal problems. Are there appropriate checks and balances in place to see that nothing is overlooked?

- Create a mission statement, a specific, reasonable set of goals, or a statement of educational philosophy, of which all stakeholders approve and agree to support. Revisit this mission and philosophy often to be sure it accurately reflects who you are.

- Expectations and responsibilities should be clear to staff as well as students. An open dialogue should be created and maintained.

- Create and use a Risk Management Advisory Committee to review goals, philosophy, venues, hiring practices, and all the workings of your program.

- Identify what qualities you desire in your instructors. Institute hiring practices that reward a wide variety of skills and experience, including local knowledge and longevity.

- Provide and encourage feedback loops among instructors. The program will benefit if clear and effective communication is present.

- Maintain your experienced instructors whenever possible. Their highest and best attribute is lost if they are not used as mentors for new instructors.

- Acquire support and understanding from your umbrella organization, if you have one. If you are part of an academic institution, be sure that your program mission is documented and accepted at all levels.

Responsible and effective risk management requires periodic and continuous re-assessment of a program's goals, philosophy, practices, and clientele, coupled with clear communication of these ever-shifting concepts among instructors/trip leaders and participants. An organization's familiar mode of operation can easily become a liability if its policies and procedures fail to keep pace with its day-to-day development. It is therefore essential that every aspect of the organization (who, what, when, where, why and how) is never taken for granted, even in the face of ongoing change.

It has been pointed out previously that "the obvious" is generally the result of hindsight, and critical self-assessment often doesn't occur until after a serious incident. Don't wait for an accident to happen before you are willing to admit that you are not immune.

Each chapter in this book approaches the management of risk from a different perspective, but all of them have common characteristics. In reading them, I've tried to imagine myself as a young leader once again, thinking back to a few different times early in my career as an educator during the 1960s. I can't help but wonder: If this book had been available to me, would I have done anything differently?

I'll start answering that question by providing a quick glance at the "arsenal" of outdoor information I had when I first began teaching. I was raised on a game farm 80 miles north of New York City. Much of my childhood was spent outdoors—alone and with siblings and friends. We fended for ourselves in the surrounding playground of hills, woods, and streams. We started skiing at an early age, having the advantage of the well-known news commentator and ski enthusiast Lowell Thomas as our mentor. Up to the time I went to college, my cellular memory was filled with information about many things in the physical environment—from plants and animals to weather and terrain, and how to determine time and distance on my own. I also learned a little about people, such as whom I could count on. My informal education was supplemented by my interest in exploration books and the opportunity to meet explorers like Peter Freuchen and Thor Heyerdal, thanks again to Lowell Thomas.

My outdoor experience increased at the University of New Hampshire. As a member of the outing club and the UNH ski team, I spent as much time in the woods, streams, and mountains of New England as possible while I worked toward my degree in English Literature. It was here that I had my first formal experiences as a leader.

The outing club was student-run. Those of us who had developed a portfolio of hiking, climbing, canoeing, sailing, hunting, fishing, woodsmanship, and general outdoor living skills became trip leaders for the novices. We had a few written guidelines for the conduct of activities, but for the most part, our judgment calls were made from the accumulation of personal experiences.

During my senior year, when I was president of the outing club, three accidents occurred, setting me off on the path that leads from the romantic to the precision stage of learning. One involved my first leader fall while rock climbing. To conserve on pitons, I did not place adequate protection, thinking, of course, that I could successfully reach a belay ledge without falling. Being 40 feet above my last piton (intermediate anchor), I fell a total of 80 feet. Because I was still at the "I'm immortal" stage of development (at least in my climbing), I am not sure I would have had the maturity to review the *Common Causes of Accidents in Outdoor Pursuits* matrix and come up with any useful insight such as, "Uh oh, inadequate protection and misperception," even if the information had been available.

For the other two accidents, however, this book might have served me well. In one case, I was co-leading a climb of New Hampshire's Mount Washington in November. We stayed at one of our outing club cabins on a Friday night, then began our climb early Saturday. The weather had deteriorated —fog and light winds—by the time we hiked the 2.4 miles up to Tuckerman Ravine, but since we had no beginners with us, we chose to go on. As we came over the lip of the bowl, we were hit by even stronger winds, plus rain and sleet. Because there was a weather observatory on the summit (where we could warm up), we decided to continue anyway.

I clearly remember two of the people in our group of about 12 showing signs of hypothermia. Both were wearing blue jeans. Had the observatory not been open, we could have had an epic on our hands. Although we knew about hypothermia, we failed to act on the information we had: wet, cold, shivering, blue lips, wanting to please others. The latter was a good part of the problem. Those who had gotten cold wanted to please us and we did not want to embarrass them by turning everyone around. Discussions about these kinds of issues beforehand would have helped and might have prevented us from getting in the predicament.

The final incident involved a spring-break ski trip to Sugarloaf in Maine. The group camped in a lower parking lot, away from the main shelter, attempting to be somewhat inconspicuous. About the third night of the trip, one of the women decided to build a snow cave in the embankment between the lower and upper lots. It was a reasonable arrangement, except that it began to rain during the night. The woman wrapped a poncho around her to serve as a waterproof layer. The weight of the rain caused the shelter to sag, which slowly sealed off her air supply. She slipped from sleep to death without any signs of a struggle.

I was not on the trip, but in my role as president, I got the phone call we all dread. Unfortunately, there was no faculty member, no advisor, no risk management committee, no support system—other than ourselves—to deal with the aftermath or help deal with the parents, media, and investigation. It was certainly not a good time for learning-by-doing. In both of these latter cases, this text would have served me well.

In my subsequent career in teaching and administration —in high school, the U.S. Army, Outward Bound, back at the University of New Hampshire, and now as a college president (on a campus that includes draft horses, chain saws, ice climbing, and a variety of other risky things)—I have had to consider the ways to reduce potential injury and damage, manage accidents when they arise, and make what I have learned available to those who may be following along these same paths.

Many of my colleagues and peers are engaged in the same process. The Wilderness Risk Managers' Committee and the annual Wilderness Risk Management Conference were born as a result of a fatal accident in 1989. Each year there is a book of "proceedings" made available at the conference for the purpose of providing participants with substantive notes to accompany the workshops they have attended. Now we have this book to provide another tool to help us conduct the important work that is being done in outdoor pursuits. Reading it has reinforced many things I know, and it has also provided some new insights.

I'll conclude with three important points, the first two of which have been addressed throughout this book:

- First, no matter how many rules, guidelines, standards, or safety nets we may have in place, unforeseen incidents will still happen.

- Second, not one of us is immune, no matter how much experience we have, how good our judgment is, or how many tools we've obtained through the years.

- Third, let us not forget that if every event is foreseen and predictable, then probably nothing very important, significant, or educational is going on. If we remove real challenges and risk, we minimize our opportunity to grow.

The best we can do is to commit ourselves to providing challenging activities that account for the capabilities of participants and are run by experienced staff who are working for well-administered programs. The goal that many have adopted is to reduce the potential for accidents that result in severe injury or fatality and yet be able to respond appropriately when they do happen.

It would not be acceptable to me personally to deprive the coming generation of students of vital lessons because we are afraid of or unwilling to expose ourselves to the level of risk that comes with the most meaningful learning in life.

So let us look to the future, learn from the past, and thank those who have created this useful set of guidelines as we pursue our learning, work, and adventures.

John E. (Jed) Williamson
President
Sterling College

Appendices
References
Author Biographies

Appendix A: Flat-Water Canoeing Course Content Guide

Course Description: Introduces the most commonly used equipment, techniques, challenges and risks found in the sport of canoeing. Includes instruction on equipment selection, trip planning, canoeing strokes and re-entry techniques with an emphasis on risk assessment and risk management.

Special Note: Requires excellent backcountry camping skills and the ability to function comfortably in inclement weather. An overnight field outing is included in the course.

Course Curriculum

1.0 Introduction to Risk Assessment and Hazard Evaluation
- 1.1 Recognizing risks inherent to the activity
  - 1.1.1 Drowning and near-drown accidents
  - 1.1.2 Water conditions
  - 1.1.3 Chop and waves
  - 1.1.4 Cold-water immersion
- 1.2 Learning to recognize environmental hazards
  - 1.2.1 Weather
  - 1.2.2 Terrain and terrain features
    - 1.2.2.1 Steep/cut banks
    - 1.2.2.2 Submerged objects
    - 1.2.2.3 Weeds, branches and trees
  - 1.2.3 Animal encounters
- 1.3 Performing a risk/benefit analysis
- 1.4 Factors that affect risk assessment
  - 1.4.1 Judgment—experience + reflection
  - 1.4.2 Team members and climbing partners
    - 1.4.2.1 As a positive influence
    - 1.4.2.2 As a negative influence
  - 1.4.3 Personal health and fitness
    - 1.4.3.1 The relationship between physical fitness and risk assessment
    - 1.4.3.2 Factors that affect physical fitness
      - 1.4.3.2.1 Rest/fatigue
      - 1.4.3.2.2 Nutrition/hydration
      - 1.4.3.2.3 Illness/injury (including hypothermia)
      - 1.4.3.2.4 Age/gender
    - 1.4.3.3 The relationship between mental/emotional health and risk assessment
    - 1.4.3.4 Factors that affect mental/emotional health
      - 1.4.3.4.1 Drugs and alcohol
      - 1.4.3.4.2 Emotions as distractions
      - 1.4.3.4.3 Relationships and group dynamics

- 1.4.4 The ability to recognize and understand personal strengths and limits
- 1.4.5 The ability to evaluate consequences, uncertainties & contingencies

2.0 Equipment
- 2.1 Canoe equipment
  - 2.1.1 Canoe types
    - 2.1.1.1 Parts of a canoe
    - 2.1.1.2 Using added flotation
  - 2.1.2 Paddles
  - 2.1.3 Painter/bow line
- 2.2 Safety equipment
  - 2.2.1 Personal flotation devices (PFDs)
    - 2.2.1.1 Types
    - 2.2.1.2 Correct sizing
  - 2.2.2 Throw ropes
- 2.3 Clothing for canoeing
- 2.4 Personal survival equipment—the 10 essentials
- 2.5 Repair kit for canoes
- 2.6 Personal vs. group first-aid kits (and waterproofing the kits)

3.0 Trip Planning
- 3.1 Setting goals
- 3.2 Identifying routes and contingencies
- 3.3 Estimating travel times
- 3.4 Assessing hazards using maps, photos, literature, etc.
- 3.5 Float plans

4.0 Transporting Your Canoe
- 4.1 Cars/trucks, trailers and planes
- 4.2 Using tie-downs
- 4.3 Portaging your canoe

5.0 Preparing to Paddle
- 5.1 Loading your canoe
- 5.2 Securing your gear
- 5.3 Flotation considerations
- 5.4 Entry/exit
  - 5.4.1 From land to canoe
  - 5.4.2 From pier to canoe
  - 5.4.3 From canoe to canoe
  - 5.4.4 Moving within the canoe

6.0 Basic Strokes
- 6.1 Forward and reverse strokes
- 6.2 Pry
- 6.3 Draw
- 6.4 J-stroke
- 6.5 Steering stroke
- 6.6 Rudder stroke

6.7 Brace
7.0 Safety Skills
7.1 Basic inner-group communication and signals
7.2 Re-entry
7.2.1 One person
7.2.2 Two person
7.2.3 Using two or more canoes
7.3 Post re-entry—basic shore-survival considerations and skills
7.3.1 Hypothermia prevention, assessment and treatment
7.3.2 Creating a safe and warm environment
7.3.3 Introduction to signaling devices
7.4 Learning to assess personal strengths and limitations
8.0 Environmental Ethics
8.1 Sanitation and waste disposal
8.2 Minimum impact
8.3 Wildlife viewing

Instructional Goals and Defined Outcomes

Introduction to Risk Assessment and Hazard Evaluation goal: Students will be able to identify the hazards most common to flat-water canoeing, such as drowning, cold-water immersion, and rough water conditions. Students will also be able to identify common environmental and subjective hazards, such as weather, terrain features and animal encounters. Students will be able to perform a basic risk-benefit analysis and will be able to identify factors that can affect risk assessment.

Equipment goal: Students will be able to identify equipment common to the sport of canoeing. This will include the different types of canoes in use, as well as the different styles of paddles. Students will also be able to identify appropriate clothing used in canoeing, safety equipment (such as personal flotation devices and throw ropes) that should be carried, repair kit items and first-aid kit items.

Trip Planning goal: Students will be able to identify the steps involved in creating a trip plan. This will include goal setting, identifying a primary and secondary trip location, assessing travel times and hazards before the trip begins, and leaving appropriate information in the float plan.

Transporting Your Canoe goal: Students will be able to identify the pros and cons of tying a canoe directly to a vehicle vs. using a trailer. They will also be able to demonstrate use of tie-downs and the proper procedure for portaging a canoe.

Preparing to Paddle goal: Students will be able to demonstrate the procedures and considerations for getting a canoe ready for use. This will include loading and securing gear while properly distributing weight. It will also include demonstrating proper entry/exit and movement within the canoe.

Basic Strokes goal: Students will be able to identify and demonstrate the types of basic strokes used in canoeing. They will also be able to describe when each would or would not be used.

Safety Skills goal: Students will be able to identify safety skills used in canoeing. This will include re-entry techniques and techniques to use once the group reaches shore. It will also include being able to assess personal and group strengths and limits.

Environmental Ethics goal: Students will be able to identify minimum impact techniques, ethical wildlife viewing practices, and sanitation and waste disposal methods appropriate to the activity and environment.

Appendix A *This course content guide provides an example of the outlines used to guide the AOEE courses. Students and instructors have found them beneficial; either as a tool when deciding what to expect in a course, or as a lesson plan for delivery.*

Appendix B: AOEE Hiring Guidelines

Instructors are hired based on skill, experience and judgment. The amount of skill and knowledge needed for an assignment will differ depending on the position (lead or assistant) and the course curriculum or activity.

LEAD INSTRUCTOR PREREQUISITES

People seeking to be lead instructors must possess a background in the following areas: technical skills specific to the course activity; extensive personal experience in the course activity; experience leading or guiding (in a paid or unpaid capacity) others in the course activity; and instructional competencies. Proof of these prerequisites can be offered by way of previous employment, personal experience, certifications and/or demonstration, depending on the prerequisite.

The following list identifies the minimum prerequisites every instructor must possess, regardless of his or her activity or environment.

Technical Skills and Personal Experience

A potential instructor needs ...

- to possess strong technical skills in his/her area of instruction. This means that the instructor's technical skills far surpass the level of technical expertise that will be taught in the specific course
- a minimum of three-years experience as an active participant in the activity s/he will be teaching (e.g., rock climbing, downhill skiing, etc.)
- to have been an active participant in the activity (s/he will be teaching) within the past two years (from the start of the course contract)
- winter skills and winter camping experience, if s/he will be leading a non-urban overnight outing

Leading or Guiding Experience

A potential instructor needs ...

- to have served as a paid or unpaid leader in the activity s/he will be teaching (or a similar activity) within the past three years (from the start of the course contract)

Instructional/Teaching Competencies

A potential instructor needs ...

- to possess college-level writing skills or higher
- experience in providing feedback and formal evaluation
- to possess good presentation and speaking skills
- experience in teaching the adult learner as well as teaching participants with various abilities and experience levels
- to possess the ability to use a variety of teaching styles

Certification/Training Requirements

A potential instructor needs ...

- to possess a current Wilderness First Responder certification if s/he will be working in a non-urban environment (i.e., two hours from definitive care)
- a current first aid/CPR certification if s/he will be working in an urban environment
- formal avalanche training within the past five years (from the start of the course contract), if s/he will be working in avalanche terrain and/or teaching avalanche hazard evaluation. This training can be from the Alaska Mountain Safety Center or a similar agency. It can also be from the AOEE program.

Appendix B *These guidelines list the basic hiring prerequisites for an AOEE instructor. Applicants must also fill out a detailed questionnaire, provide a letter of recommendation, and provide three references as part of the hiring/selection process. Cumulatively, these prerequisites reflect the instructor skills Simon Priest identifies in Chapter Two.*

Appendix C: Volunteer Responsibilities

The volunteer's responsibilities regarding course content and information dissemination:
The volunteer is not expected to do any of the teaching during a classroom session or outing. In the event that a lead instructor (LI) would like the volunteer to teach a subject or skill, the LI should clearly communicate expectations and the topic/duties should be prearranged.

The volunteer's responsibilities before, during and after an outing:
- review the AOEE policy and procedure manual and follow all AOEE field policies and procedures
- communicate with the LI before each outing in order to receive the instructor's approval (to attend an outing) and discuss field roles and expectations
- carry personal survival and safety equipment during all outings
- role model excellent behavior in the area of personal care during all outings
- role model excellent risk assessment and risk management behaviors
- contribute to an atmosphere of open communication, with the instructors and the students, during all field outings
- complete all field duties that have been delegated by the LI or the assistant instructor
- seek feedback from the LI regarding his/her performance

The volunteer may be asked to assist the instructors in overseeing the field safety (physical and emotional) of all employees, volunteers and participants.

The volunteer's responsibilities at the end of a course:
- provide a written evaluation of the instructors at the end of the course

If the volunteer has attended more than one outing during a course, s/he is expected to meet with the LI in order to debrief the course.

Appendix C *This basic list clearly identifies what is expected of AOEE volunteers and reduces the chance of assumptions or misunderstandings. In addition, AOEE requires that volunteers have a minimum amount of training and experience, and volunteers are required to attend a program orientation before they are allowed to work in the field.*

Appendix D: Policy and Accepted Field Practice

TRAVELING IN AVALANCHE TERRAIN

In AOEE courses, avalanche terrain is considered a snowy slope that is 20 degrees or more in slope angle. If a slope (snowy or not) of any angle is adjacent to or below a snowy slope of 20 degrees or more, the terrain is considered potentially hazardous.

All AOEE instructors who will be traveling in avalanche terrain (or teaching Level I courses) are required to be skilled and knowledgeable in hazard evaluation and rescue techniques.

Lead instructors are required to have formal avalanche training, preferably a three-day workshop, before they work in avalanche terrain. Assistant instructors must have received at least a full day of training before they are allowed to work in avalanche terrain. Instructors/assistants must attend at least a full-day refresher at least every three years. Each employee's training history will be kept in his/her personnel file.

Level I courses include Mountaineering I, II, III and Expedition Mountaineering; Skiing Alaska's Backcountry; Backcountry Snowboarding; Four-Season Backpacking; Alaska Winter Survival; and Expedition Glacier School.

All AOEE instructors who might encounter avalanche terrain (or who are teaching Level II courses) are required to be knowledgeable in avalanche hazard evaluation.

In certain AOEE courses, it is unlikely but possible that the group will encounter avalanche terrain. Lead instructors of those courses are required to have had avalanche hazard evaluation training prior to teaching.

Level II courses include Outdoor Adventure in Alaska; Nature Observation and Tracking; Ice Climbing; Crevasse Rescue Techniques; Cross-Country Skiing, Diagonal Stride; Cross-Country Skate Skiing; Introduction to Telemark Skiing; Introduction to Snowboarding; Introduction to Alpine Skiing; Introduction to Winter Camping; and Dog Mushing.

When it is anticipated that a class could be traveling in avalanche terrain, all participants are required to carry an inclinometer, an avalanche beacon, a shovel and a probe. Participants are not allowed to enter the terrain unless every member is in possession of the above items and the instructor has had formal training in avalanche hazard evaluation and rescue techniques.

Transceivers must be checked and turned on before participants enter any avalanche terrain. They must remain on until the group is completely out of any danger. Extra batteries and an extra transceiver(s) should be carried with large groups or on expedition courses.

Before a group enters avalanche terrain, participants must receive training on avalanche hazard evaluation and rescue techniques.

Participants must know how to use the equipment they are carrying. They must also be trained regarding techniques that might help in the event they are caught in an avalanche.

In courses that will be traveling in avalanche terrain, a weather forecast must be obtained before the group enters the field.

The Anchorage and vicinity forecast can be obtained by calling the National Weather Forecast at 266-5105. A recorded message can be obtained by calling 936-2525. Additional information regarding an area's history can be obtained by contacting the AOEE office, the Department of Transportation (243-7675), the Alaska Railroad (265-2403), Alaska State Parks (345-5014) and/or the Chugach National Forest (271-2500)

Appendix D *These instructions provide an example of AOEE policies regarding travel in avalanche terrain. Instructors are given parameters regarding training minimums and required equipment, but they are not told* how *to cross potentially hazardous slopes.*

Appendix E: Feedback Loops

Student evaluation of an instructor:

- How would you rate this (lead) instructor's overall performance?
- Did you feel free to say something if/when you were uncomfortable?
- How receptive was the instructor to questions/comments/concerns from the students regarding safety, judgment or decisions that were made?
- How satisfied were you with information/answers that were given?
- How sensitive was the instructor to the students' safety and well-being?
- How sensitive was the instructor to his or her own safety and well-being?
- Please identify an area or areas where this instructor could improve.
- What types of behavior did the instructor role model particularly well?

Questions for instructors and supervisors:

- How open to student feedback – regarding style, content or skills – was this instructor?
- How receptive was the instructor to questions/comments/confrontation from the students regarding his/her judgment or decisions?
- How receptive was the instructor to your constructive criticism?
- How would you rate this instructor's listening skills?
- How sensitive was the instructor to the students' safety and well-being?
- How sensitive was the instructor to your safety and well-being?
- How sensitive was the instructor to his or her own safety and well-being?
- How closely did this instructor stick to the course curriculum identified in the CCG?
- Please identify an area or areas where this instructor could improve.
- What types of behavior did the instructor role model particularly well?

Evaluating an instructor's knowledge of and ability to teach course content:

- Risk Assessment and Hazard Evaluation
- Personal Clothing and Safety Equipment
- Knots and Hitches
- Belay Techniques
- Climbing Techniques
- Descent Techniques

Evaluating the course and course objectives:

- How closely do you think you came to meeting the course objectives identified on the syllabus?
- Did the course outcomes (what you were taught and what you learned) meet your expectations?
- Please identify the best/worst thing about the venue (field location) used. If you had more than one outing, please identify the best/worst venue used.
- Do you believe the venue(s) used was appropriate to the skills taught and the experience level of participants? Why or why not?
- How well did this course prepare you to recognize the risks inherent in this activity? To assess the risks? To minimize the risks?

Appendix E *This list provides multiple examples of the questions that are used in the on-going feedback loops AOEE has incorporated into its programming. By asking a variety of questions, as compared to the typical participant satisfaction feedback that is generally gathered in other programs, the department is able to evaluate its curriculum, instructors, venues and risk management practices on an ongoing basis.*

Appendix F: Serious Incident/Accident Review Process

I. Preparation and Understanding

There are some givens that need to be understood before looking at what happens when a serious incident occurs in your program.

- Following a major incident, internal and often times external reviews are a common practice in all industries.
- All programs should have a Risk Management Committee, and each member should clearly understand the Emergency Action Plan and External Review process.
- There should be a clear understanding and agreement among program administration, board of directors, insurance carrier, and legal counsel regarding the post incident review process. (Issues may include unwillingness of insurance carrier to include outside reviewers, levels of disclosure to family, other outside interests, etc.)

II. When to Consider an External Review of an Incident

- When a fatality occurs to a participant
- When a fatality occurs to a staff member while on duty
- When a permanently disabling injury occurs to a participant
- (Possibly) when a permanently disabling injury occurs to a staff member while on duty
- (Possibly) when a life threatening injury occurs to a participant or staff member (while on duty)

III. What is the Role of an External Review Team?

- Overall Mission: to help the industry prevent fatalities and permanently disabling injuries.
- Specific Mission: to help the program find and/or confirm the primary and secondary causes of the incident.
- Goal: to provide recommendations and suggestions that focus on prevention of further incidents and improvement of quality; i.e., to serve as a consultant.
- Hazard: members of the team may be asked to become expert witnesses – by either side!

IV. Who Should Be on an External Review Team?

Personality:

- Select members who are empathetic, open minded, reflective, have proven communication skills (verbal and written), and are able to maintain objectivity and confidentiality.
- Do not select persons who may have a conflict of interest, who are known to have biases, and who may already have formed an opinion.

Skills:

- The team leader should have, in addition to the above, credibility in the field, including several seasons of direct instruction and at least three years of administrative experience.
- At least one member should have unquestionable expertise in the activity and type of terrain in which the incident occurred.

- Other factors will determine what other kinds of skill sets are needed. For example, appoint a doctor if a medical condition (illness, hypothermia, dehydration, HAPE, etc.) was part of the cause; appoint a school administrator if the incident occurred on a school outing; appoint a counselor/psychologist if participants were from a special population.

V. Ground Rules for an External Review Team

- Assure program that findings will be confidential unless otherwise agreed.
- Secure understanding from program that the review team will be operating independently, and that its findings will be based on the facts discovered.
- Get agreement from program that all records and people will be available to the review team.
- Get agreement from the program that all recommendations will be followed.
- Assure that support will be provided as needed.
- Media: discuss and agree on how media will be handled, including when final. report is released. No matter what, no talking with the media before the end of the process. Be explicit about book, article, movie, TV requests.
- Agree in writing as to fees and costs.
- If a conflict arises among team members, it will be resolved in private, with the team leader having the ultimate authority.

VI. Steps in Conducting an External Review of an Incident

1) The program should begin appointing the review team immediately following the incident. There should be a team leader, and from two to five other members, depending on the magnitude and kind of incident.

2) Draw up a written agreement as to scope of work, process, costs, and distribution of the final report.

3) External review team steps:

- Team leader communicates with other members as to the timing, process, tasks and assignments.
- When environmental factors are part of the cause, deploy at least one review team member to the site ASAP (before conditions change). Photographs, and perhaps video, of the scene should be part of this process.
- Review all pertinent written materials.
- Conduct site visits, including spot where incident occurred.
- Interview appropriate administration, staff, and external people and agencies involved.
- Each team member writes findings. Team leader writes draft for the program's risk management committee or internal review team.
- Team leader meets with program's team to discuss draft and possible revisions.
- Team leader submits final report to designated program person(s).
- Team leader should be available for meetings with various levels of program to discuss final report.

Foreword

Senge, P. (1990). The fifth discipline: The art and practice of the learning organization. New York: Doubleday.

Introduction

Wade, I. (1999). Risk management course. Paper presented at the Wilderness Risk Management Conference, Sierra Vista, AZ.

Chapter One

Geis, C. (1984). Human factors in investigation. Los Angeles, CA: University of Southern California Press.

Gookin, J. (1998). Defining and developing judgment. Paper presented in the Wilderness Risk Management Conference Proceedings, Black Mountain, NC.

Green, R., & Doran, M. (1998). Decision-making for students. Paper presented in the Wilderness Risk Management Conference Proceedings, Black Mountain, NC.

Haddock, C. (1999). Epic lies and hero stories: the folklore of near misses in the outdoors. Paper presented in the Wilderness Risk Management Conference Proceedings, Sierra Vista, AZ.

Hawkins, F. (1987). Human factors in flight. Aldershot, England: Gower Technical Press.

Leemon, D. (Ed.)(1998). Adventure program risk management report: incident data and narratives from 1991–1997. Boulder, CO: Association for Experiential Education.

Leemon, D. (May, 1999). A review of leading types and causes of incidents on NOLS courses: injury, illness and near miss profiles. NOLS Newsletter; Special Edition Highlighting Risk Management, 4-7.

Perrow, C. (1984). Normal accidents: Living with high risk technologies. Princeton, NJ: Princeton University Press.

Reason, J. (1991). Identifying the latent causes of aircraft accidents before and after the event. Paper presented at the ISASI Forum Proceedings.

Sagan, S. D. (1995). The limits of safety: Organizations, accidents, and nuclear weapons. Princeton, NJ: Princeton University Press.

Schimelpfenig, T. (1997). Teaching safety awareness. Paper presented in the Wilderness Risk Management Conference Proceedings, Snowbird, UT.

Thompson, D. (1999). Operational risk management. Torrance, CA: Southern California Safety Institute.

Williamson, J. (1997). Understanding the meaning of risk. Paper presented in the Wilderness Risk Management Conference Proceedings, Snowbird, UT.

Williamson, J. (1999). Potential causes of accidents in outdoor pursuits. Paper presented in the Wilderness Risk Management Conference Proceedings, Sierra Vista, AZ.

Wood, R. (1988). The definition of aircraft accident causes. Paper presented at the ISASI Forum Proceedings.

Chapter Two

Buell, L. H. (1981). The identification of outdoor adventure leadership competencies for entry-level and experience-level personnel. Unpublished doctoral dissertation, University of Massachusetts.

Furlong, L., Jillings, A., LaRhette, M. & Ryan, B. (1995). 20-year safety study. Hamilton, MA: Project Adventure.

Green, P. J. (1981). The content of a college-level outdoor leadership course for land-based outdoor pursuits in the Pacific Northwest: a Delphi consensus. Unpublished doctoral dissertation, University of Oregon.

Hale, A. (1983). Safety management for outdoor program leaders. Unpublished manuscript.

Higgins, L. (1981). Wilderness schools: risk vs. danger. The Physician and Sports Medicine, 9(3), 133-136.

Kahneman, D., Slovic, P. and Tversky, A. (1982). Judgment under uncertainty: Heuristics and biases. New York: Cambridge University Press.

KPMG Peat Marwick. (1997). State of the industry report: Human powered outdoor recreation. Boulder, CO: The Outdoor Recreation Coalition of America; and North Palm Beach, FL: The Sporting Goods Manufacturers Association.

Meyer, D. (1979). The management of risk. The Journal of Experiential Education, 2(2), 9-14.

Petzoldt, P. (1984). The new wilderness handbook. New York: W.W. Norton & Company, Inc.

Priest, S. (1984). Effective outdoor leadership: a survey. Journal of Experiential Education, 7(3), 34-36.

Priest, S. (1986). Outdoor leadership in five nations. Unpublished doctoral dissertation, University of Oregon.

Priest, S. (1987). Preparing effective outdoor pursuit leaders. Eugene, OR: Institute of Recreation Research and Service.

Priest, S. & Baillie, R. (1987). Justifying the risk to others: the real razor's edge. Journal of Experiential Education, 10(1), 16-22.

Priest, S. (1988). The role of judgment, decision making, and problem solving for outdoor leaders. Journal of Experiential Education, 11(3), 19-26.

Priest, S. (1990). Everything you always wanted to know about judgment, but were afraid to ask. Journal of Adventure Education and Outdoor Leadership, 7(3), 5-12.

Priest, S. & Gass, M. A. (1998). Effective leadership in adventure programming. Champaign, IL: Human Kinetics.

Raiola, E. O. (1986). Outdoor wilderness education - a leadership curriculum. Unpublished doctoral dissertation, Union Graduate School.

Swiderski, M. J. (1981). Outdoor leadership competencies identified by outdoor leaders in five western regions. Unpublished doctoral dissertation, University of Oregon.

Williamson, J., Ratz, J. & Miller, D. (1997, December 9). Review team report: Alaska Wilderness Studies program — Ptarmigan Peak incident of June 29, 1997. Anchorage, AK: Chancellor's Office, University of Alaska.

Foreword

by Dr. Daniel M. Johnson

Dan Johnson is the provost at the University of Alaska Anchorage. Prior to his current position, Mr. Johnson was Dean of the School of Community Service at the University of North Texas in Denton, Texas, a position he held for six years. During his tenure at the University of North Texas, Mr. Johnson served on numerous boards and commissions. Governors Ann Richards and George W. Bush both appointed him to membership on the Texas Commission on Community and National Service, the state oversight group for volunteerism and the Americorp program. He was also recipient of the University of North Texas Equal Opportunity Award for his leadership in bringing greater diversity to the faculty, staff and student body. Mr. Johnson received his B.A. and M.A. from Texas Christian University and earned his Ph.D. from the University of Missouri-Columbia.

Chapter One: How Accidents Happen

by Drew Leemon and Scott Erickson

Drew Leemon is the risk management director at the National Outdoor Leadership School (NOLS) in Lander, Wyoming. He is a senior NOLS field instructor and has extensive experience in the western U.S. and Alaska. Mr. Leemon leads the Wilderness Risk Managers' Committee and is committed to encouraging and advancing open dialogue regarding risk management and field practices among outdoor and adventure-based programs.

Scott Erickson is employed full time as an air safety investigator with the National Transportation Safety Board (NTSB). He has been with the NTSB since 1991, and has been assigned to Alaska since 1995. Prior to 1991, Mr. Erickson was employed as a police officer in Tucson, AZ. Mr. Erickson also works part time as an adjunct faculty member for the University of Alaska Anchorage's outdoor education department, and is a member of the Alaska Mountain Rescue Group and Mountaineering Club of Alaska.

Chapter Two: Effective Outdoor Leadership

by Dr. Simon Priest

Simon Priest is the leading researcher and writer in experiential training and development with corporations. He presently provides consultation in facilitation training, leadership enhancement, and executive development for a handful of progressive companies interested in staying ahead of their global competition by focusing on the development and maintenance of human resource relationships. Now early retired, he maintains adjunct professorships at several universities and management institutes around the world. His two latest books are *101 of the Best Corporate Team Building Activities* with Karl Rohnke and *The Essential Elements of Facilitation* with Mike Gass and Lee Gillis.

Chapter Three: Learning from Ptarmigan Peak—Rewriting an Organizational Risk Management Plan

by Deborah L. Ajango

Deb Ajango has been the coordinator of the University of Alaska Anchorage's academic outdoor program since June 1997. She is a member of the Association for Experiential Education's Accreditation Council, is on the board of the Alaska Wilderness Recreation & Tourism Association, and has provided risk management consultation in Alaska and the Lower 48. Ms. Ajango has more than 12 years experience teaching mountaineering, backpacking and paddling in Alaska's backcountry, and she has traveled throughout the continental United States, Canada, Mexico, South America, Africa, Australia and New Zealand.

Chapter Four: The Jury's In—A Defense Lawyer's Perspective on Risk Management and Crisis Response

by R. Eldridge (Bob) Hicks
with an addendum by Charles (Reb) Gregg

Bob Hicks is a practicing attorney educated at Harvard Law School (1971) and Stanford University (1968). His legal career focuses on diving law, maritime law, and defense litigation. Mr. Hicks is an active dive instructor, hyperbaric chamber technician, cave/wreck diver and scientific diver. He counsels dive businesses and diving organizations in risk management, incident management, and business planning to limit liability.

Reb Gregg is a partner in the Houston, Texas, firm of Locke, Liddell & Sapp LLP, where he specializes in commercial litigation. His practice includes representation and consultation regarding legal issues in adventure programs. He has served for many years as general counsel to the National Outdoor Leadership School, and his clients include a variety of recreational and educational outdoor programs throughout the country. Mr. Gregg serves on the Wilderness Risk Managers' Committee, the Accreditation Council of the Association for Experiential Education, and the Editorial Board of The Outdoor Network. He lectures and writes frequently on legal issues pertaining to the outdoor industry.

Chapter Five: The Role of the Media in Accident Response

by Ty Hardt

Ty Hardt has 10 years experience in the Anchorage television market, specializing in environmental and outdoor reporting. He has won local Goldie and Press Club awards and is currently news director of Anchorage's ABC affiliate. Mr. Hardt was one of the first reporters on the scene after the Ptarmigan Peak accident, and during the past two and a half years he has re-traced the route, followed the numerous legal claims, anniversaries, reviews, re-structuring and re-naming of the outdoor department, and even accompanied the program's first mountaineering class back into the hills.

Chapter Six: Ethical Foundations of Wilderness Risk Management

by Dr. Jasper S. Hunt Jr.

Jasper Hunt is professor of Leadership Studies and Experiential Education and director of Adventure Education Programs in the Department of Educational Leadership at Minnesota State University. His background includes extensive field experience as a senior Outward Bound instructor. Mr. Hunt's Ph.D. is from the University of Colorado Boulder.

Chapter Seven: The Importance of Ongoing Assessment

by William L. Ennis and Constance E. Livsey

Bill Ennis has been an adjunct instructor for University of Alaska's outdoor education department since 1982, and is presently the program's senior mountaineering instructor. He is also a full-time physics teacher in Anchorage, and was the winner of the British Petroleum Alaska Teacher of the Year (1996) and Milken Family Foundation (1999) awards.

Conni Livsey has been both student and instructor in the University of Alaska's outdoor program and is presently the lead instructor for the department's Introduction to Sailing course. She is a partner with the law firm of Holmes, Weddle, & Barcott, where she supervises the workers' compensation practice group and represents and advises employers and insurers in a variety of matters. She has served as counsel to the Anchorage Equal Rights Commission since 1989, and was appointed by Governor Knowles to the Alaska State Medical Board in 1997.

Mr. Ennis and Ms. Livsey are members of the Alaska Outdoor & Experiential Education Risk Management Advisory Committee.

Afterword

by John E. (Jed) Williamson

Jed Williamson is currently the president of Sterling College in Vermont. Mr. Williamson has co-authored the Association for Experiential Education's *Accreditation Standards for Adventure Programs*, has been involved with more than 100 safety and quality reviews around the country, has been the editor of *Accidents in North American Mountaineering* since 1974, and has published several articles and produced three educational videos on experiential and adventure topics. His outdoor background includes more than 40 years of climbing and skiing, and 10 years working as an instructor and administrator for Outward Bound.